CU00558729

Celebrating
The Word

Celebrating the Word

Complete Services of The Word
for use with Common Worship and the
Church of Ireland Book of Common Prayer

Compiled and edited
by Brian Mayne

CANTERBURY
PRESS
Norwich

Celebrating the Word
is published by **Canterbury Press Norwich**
a publishing imprint of Hymns Ancient & Modern Limited,
a registered charity,
St Mary's Works, St Mary's Plain, Norwich, Norfolk, NR3 3BH

Compiled and edited by Brian Mayne

Published 2004

A catalogue record for this book is available
from the British Library.

ISBN 1-85311-607-6

Printed & Bound in Great Britain by
Biddles Ltd, Kings Lynn, Norfolk

Dedicated

to the people who first used services in this book

and made forms of service into worship,

offered to Almighty God

in the Cathedral of the Holy Trinity, Down
Downpatrick, County Down

and in the parish churches of the Lecale Group

between 1993 and 2001.

CONTENTS

Abbreviations in references to hymns:

CH   Church Hymnal 5th edition © 2000 Oxford University Press
               the normal hymnbook of the Church of Ireland
CP   Common Praise © 2000 Canterbury Press

INTRODUCTION

In the early years of the 1990s quite independently the Churches of England and Ireland found themselves planning a similar flexible order of service which could be shaped to suit many different situations and draw on a variety of resources. Each Liturgy Commission learned from the other but the final results had a distinct family relationship.

Although at first planned for 'family' or 'all-age' worship, time proved that the formula could be used for a variety of situations from Christian Aid Week to the Mothers' Union Diocesan Festival. Under provisions in its constitution the Church of Ireland issued a booklet with four 'worked-out' forms and some resources for trial use. Subsequently provisions for A Service of the Word were included in the 2004 revision of the Church of Ireland *Book of Common Prayer*. Slightly stricter rules were formalized in 2000 in *Common Worship: Services and Prayers for the Church of England*.

The services in this book are mostly based on forms of Service of the Word which follow the guidelines of the Church of Ireland Prayer Book. These I compiled and used over a seven year period in the Lecale Group of Parishes in the diocese of Down in Northern Ireland. That explains why there is no specific service for the season of Lent as during that season we would be using the service for Mothering Sunday and from 1994 the service for Palm Sunday. A few of the forms have been developed by other clergy in the Church of Ireland and I am grateful to them for sharing them with me and allowing me to tweak them into a fairly consistent shape.

In some services specific hymns, scripture songs and readings are specified. These happen to be ones that were appropriate to the occasion for the congregations at the time. Anyone who chooses to use any of these services is free to adapt them to their own needs. In other services these elements are left to the discretion of the worship planner.

For this book I have changed the titles of the distinct elements in the service from those set out in the Church of Ireland *Book of Common Prayer* to make them more positive – Gathering, Responding, Going out as God's People. It will be noted that the affirmation of faith is part of our Responding unlike the Church of England outline where it is part of the Liturgy of the Word.

If the services are used in the Church of England the confession, absolution and affirmation of faith must be according to authorised forms set out in Common Worship.

BRIAN MAYNE
Downpatrick, Co Down

GUIDELINES

The following extract from the 2004 edition of the Church of Ireland Book of Common Prayer sets out the governing rules for the services which follow in this book.

SERVICE OF THE WORD

THE STRUCTURE OF THE SERVICE

Preparation
* A liturgical Greeting
  An invitation to worship
  A hymn may be sung.
* Penitence may be at this part of the service or in Response.
* An Acclamation and/or a Song of praise
  Metrical forms of canticles may be used, or a hymn may be sung.
* The Collect of the day

Ministry of the Word
* Readings from the Bible
* A Psalm and/or a Scripture Song may precede or follow readings.
  A Bible Responsory may follow a reading.
* The Sermon
  A hymn may be sung.

Response
* An Affirmation of Faith
  The Apostles' Creed, the Nicene Creed, the Affirmation of Faith from the Renewal of Baptismal Vows or a scriptural Affirmation of Faith.
* The Prayers
        Intercessions and Thanksgiving
        Penitence (if not used above)
        A general collect
  The whole section is concluded with The Lord's Prayer.
   A hymn may be sung.

Dismissal
* A dismissal prayer
  Blessing
  A salutation

*Sections marked with * are mandatory in any service based on this structure.*

NOTES

Service of the Word is for use on occasions when the prescribed services of Morning and Evening Prayer or Holy Communion may not meet the needs of a particular congregation.

A basic structure for all such services is provided.

Examples of working out that structure approved by the House of Bishops have been published. Resource material authorised by the House of Bishops such as *New Patterns for Worship* (Church House Publishing 2002) or *Common Worship: Times and Seasons* (Church House Publishing 2004) may be used to work out other forms based on the Structure.

1 The Structure has four sections:

Preparation:

A Greeting, an invitation to worship, a hymn of praise to God, an act of penitence (but this may on occasion be more appropriate in the section called Response) and an Acclamation.

The Collect of the day is the climax of the Preparation and leads in to the Ministry of the Word.

Ministry of the Word: The Reading and exposition of Holy Scripture is the central part of the service. The use of the Psalms whether sung in metrical versions, or chanted or recited from the Psalter, enables the congregation to interact with the Readings. Periods of silence also help this interaction. The use of Scripture Songs ('canticles') is recommended.

Response: Normally an Affirmation of Faith is followed by prayers for the Church and for the World. Sometimes penitence is also appropriate if not used in the Preparation. After a General Collect the climax of this section comes as the congregation says together the Lord's Prayer. In this section the Offering may come before or after the Prayers.

The service ends with The Dismissal. Either a Dismissal Prayer or a Blessing may be followed by a final salutation.

2 The keynote of Service of the Word is simplicity. It should not have a complicated opening. The service begins with a Greeting and Invitation to worship. This governs the choice of any hymn to be sung at this point.

3 Penitence will normally be expressed in the Preparation.

4 The Acclamation is a proclamation of God's majesty and love that derives from the Greeting and Invitation. Traditional elements like the Sursum Corda and Sanctus, as well as Canticles such as Gloria in Excelsis may have a place here.

5 The Collect of the day is given a special position, similar to its use in the Communion Service: the climax of the Preparation. It is the 'link' with all the other worship of the Church on the day. It may be introduced with a 'one-line' bidding, deriving from the central thrust of the prayer.

6 Psalms and what are entitled Scripture Songs are vital components of the Service. Metrical versions of some Psalms are to be found in *Church Hymnal*. Other sources of psalmody and different ways of using it can be explored.

7 There should be at least two Readings from the Bible. Normally the Sunday lectionary will determine the selection. On occasion readings may be presented in dramatised form.

8 The use of the terminology, The Sermon, the legally recognized word in the Church of Ireland, does not rule out a variety of ways of proclaiming the message of the Gospel; these may include drama, interviews and other techniques.

9 When appropriate the Sermon may be followed by a hymn. An Affirmation of Faith is regarded as essential. On some occasions it might be deemed suitable for an act of penitence to precede the Affirmation of Faith in the Response.

10 The section containing the Prayers should conclude with a General Collect. The climax of the Prayers, indeed of the whole Response, is the Lord's Prayer, with an appropriate introduction.

11 The service ends with the Dismissal. If a concluding hymn is customary it is better for this to precede the Blessing and final salutation.

12 Periods of silence are important. Some indications of where these are most suitable have been given. Care and instruction are needed so that worshippers can learn how to use silence in worship.

The equivalent material in *Common Worship: Services and Prayers for the Church of England* is on pages 21-27 of that book.

1 GENERAL Form A

The first three forms of Service of the Word are those published by the Liturgical Advisory Committee in 1993 to illustrate ways of putting together such services. For this book the section headings have been amended for consistency.

GATHERING

Greeting
The Peace of the Lord be always with you
and also with you.

Members of the congregation may greet one another with a sign of peace.

The Lord is my strength and my song:
He has become my salvation

Sing to the Lord, for he has done glorious things:
Let it be known in all the world.

A hymn is sung.

Penitence

Let us kneel and recall our disobedience to God's commandments and our failure to do his will; and let us confess our sins to God our Father:
Almighty God, our heavenly Father,
we have sinned in thought and word and deed,
through negligence, through weakness,
through our own deliberate fault.
We are truly sorry and repent of all our sins.
For the sake of your Son Jesus Christ who died for us,
forgive us all that is past;
and grant that we may serve you in newness of life
to the glory of your name. Amen.

The priest pronounces the absolution.
Almighty God, who forgives all who truly repent,
have mercy on you,
pardon and deliver you from all sins,
confirm and strengthen you in all goodness,
and keep you in eternal life;
through Jesus Christ our Lord. **Amen.**

If no priest is present the absolution is omitted and the following prayer may be said:
Merciful Lord,
grant to your faithful people pardon and peace,
that we may be cleansed from all our sins,
and serve you with a quiet mind;
through Jesus Christ our Lord. **Amen.**

Acclamation
Stand

Lift up your hearts.
We lift them to the Lord.

Let us give thanks to the Lord our God.
It is right to give our thanks and praise.

We give you thanks, our God and Father,
for you have created us and you sustain us.
Through your only Son Jesus Christ
you have revealed your love and your care for all your people;
you are ready to forgive and to save in time of need;
so we proclaim your glory, saying
Holy, holy, holy Lord,
God of power and might,
Heaven and earth are full of your glory.
Hosanna in the highest.

The Collect of the day

MINISTRY OF THE WORD

*A **Psalm** is said or sung.*

Readings
One or more Scripture readings, each may be followed by a short time of silence.

Scripture Song
God we praise you, (CH 696; CP 450) is suitable.

The Sermon

RESPONDING

Affirmation of Faith

Do you believe and trust in God the Father?
**I believe in God, the Father Almighty,
creator of heaven and earth.**

Do you believe and trust in his Son Jesus Christ?
**I believe in Jesus Christ, God's only Son, our Lord
who redeemed us and all the world.**

Do you believe and trust in the Holy Spirit?
**I believe in the Holy Spirit
who gives life to us and all the people of God.**

This is the faith of the Church.
**This is our faith.
We believe and trust in one God,
Father, Son, and Holy Spirit.**

Prayers

Gracious and loving God,
we thank you for giving us power through your Spirit
to reveal your life to the world.
Strengthen, bless and guide us to make you known by word and
example...
We are your Church, Lord.
Guide us in your grace.

We thank you for your creation,
and pray for the earth you have given us to cherish and protect.
Nourish us in your love for all you have made...
We are your stewards, Lord.
Guide us in your grace.

Guide and bless us in our work and in our play,
and shape the patterns of our country's political and economic life,
that all may share in the fulfilment of your creative work...
We are your servants, Lord.
Guide us in your grace.

Awaken our hearts to your presence in all people:
in those we love; in those whom we find difficult it to love,
in those who differ from us and those who are familiar to us...
We are made in your image, Lord.
Guide us in your grace.

We thank you for the gift of life, with its blessings and its sorrows.
Shield the joyous, comfort and strengthen those in any need or
trouble, especially ...
Bless those who will be born today and those who will die,
joining in the company of all your saints,
that we may rejoice in one unending song of praise...

> In you alone we have eternal life, Lord.
> **Guide us in your grace.**

Through Jesus Christ our Lord
we offer these our prayers and thanksgivings to you, Lord God,
source of all that is true and holy, now and for ever. **Amen.**

A general collect
Eternal God and Father,
you create us by your power
and redeem us by your love:
Guide and strengthen us by your Spirit,
that we may give ourselves in love and service
to one another and to you;
through Jesus Christ our Lord. Amen.

Let us sum up our prayers and praises in the words our Saviour
Christ has taught us and say:

> **Our Father...**

A hymn may be sung.

GOING OUT AS GOD'S PEOPLE

Grant, O Lord, that as we leave your house
we may not leave your presence:
be ever near us and keep us close to you
now and for ever. **Amen.**

Blessing
The Lord bless you and keep you.
Amen.
The Lord make his face shine on you and be gracious to you.
Amen.
The Lord lift up his countenance upon you and give you peace.
Amen.
The Lord Almighty, Father, Son, and Holy Spirit,
Holy and Undivided Trinity
guard you, save you and bring you to the heavenly city
where he lives and reigns for ever and ever. **Amen.**

2 GENERAL Form B

GATHERING

Greeting

Come close to God, and he will come close to you.   *James 4:8*

The Lord our God is worthy to receive glory and honour and power, for he has redeemed us.   *Revelation 4:11; 5:9*

Heavenly Father,
in our worship help us to sing your praise,
confess our sins,
hear your word
and bring our prayers to you,
through Jesus Christ our Lord. **Amen.**

A hymn is sung.

Penitence

If we say we have no sin we deceive ourselves,
and the truth is not in us.
If we confess our sins, God is faithful and just
and will forgive our sins and cleanse us from all unrighteousness.
1 John 1:8,9

Let us kneel and confess our sins to God our Father.

Almighty God, our Father,
we come to you in sorrow and humility to confess our sins:

For turning away from you, and ignoring your will for our lives:
Father, forgive us,
Save us and help us.

For behaving just as we wish, without thinking of you:
Father, forgive us,
Save us and help us.

For failing you — not only by what we have done,
but also by our thoughts and by what we have said:
Father, forgive us,
Save us and help us.

For letting ourselves be drawn away from you by
temptations in the world about us:
Father, forgive us,
Save us and help us.

For acting as if we are ashamed to belong
to your dear Son Christ Jesus:

Father, forgive us,
Save us and help us.

Father, we have failed you often,
we humbly ask your forgiveness
and your help so to live that others may see your glory;
through Jesus Christ our Lord. **Amen**.

Acclamation
Stand
Praise the Lord, O my soul,
and all that is within me, praise his holy Name.

Praise the Lord, O my soul,
and forget not all his benefits.

He forgives all your sin
and heals all your infirmities.

The Lord is full of compassion and mercy,
slow to anger and of great goodness.

As far as the east is from the west:
so far has he set our sins from us.

Glory to the Father and to the Son, and to the Holy Spirit;
as it was in the beginning, is now, and shall be for ever. Amen.

The Collect of the day

MINISTRY OF THE WORD

First Reading
This may be followed by a short time of silence.

Scripture Song
All Created Things (CH 682) is suitable.

Second Reading

Bible Responsory
Lord, your steadfast love never ceases.
Your mercies never come to an end.

They are new every morning; great is your faithfulness.
Your mercies never come to an end.

Glory to the Father, and to the Son, and to the Holy Spirit.
Your mercies never come to an end.

The Sermon

RESPONDING

Stand

Affirmation of Faith

The Apostles' Creed is said.

A hymn is sung.

The Prayers

Intercessions, Petitions and Thanksgivings in the form of bidding, silence and collect type prayer.

A general collect

**God,
you make us glad with the weekly remembrance
of the glorious resurrection of your Son, our Lord Jesus Christ:
Give us such blessing through our worship of you this day,
that the week to come may be spent in your favour;
through Jesus Christ our Lord. Amen.**

Gathering all our prayers and praises into one,
we pray as our Saviour Christ has taught us:
> **Our Father...**

A hymn may be sung and when the collection is received this prayer may be said by the minister or by all:

**Accept, Lord, these our gifts,
and use them for your purposes of love;
through Jesus Christ our Lord. Amen.**

GOING OUT AS GOD'S PEOPLE

May our Lord Jesus Christ himself,
and God our Father,
who loved us and graciously gave us
eternal encouragement and good hope,
encourage our hearts and strengthen us
in every good deed and word. **Amen.** *2 Thessalonians 2:16,17*

Let us go in the Name of Christ.
Thanks be to God.

3   GENERAL Form C

GATHERING

Greeting

This is the day that the Lord has made:
We will rejoice and be glad in it.

Lord, direct our thoughts,
help us to pray,
and lift up our hearts to worship you
in Spirit and in truth,
through Jesus Christ our Lord. **Amen.**

The Spirit of God fills the whole world:
Come, let us worship.

A hymn is sung.

Penitence

If we say we have no sin we deceive ourselves,
and the truth is not in us.
If we confess our sins, God is faithful and just
and will forgive our sins and cleanse us
from all unrighteousness. *1 John 1: 8,9*

Let us kneel and confess our sins to God our Father.

**O God, our loving Father in heaven,
we confess that we have sinned against you;
we have broken your commandments;
we have often been selfish,
and we have not loved you as we should.
For these, and all our sins,
forgive us, we pray;
through our Lord and Saviour Jesus Christ. Amen.**

A priest pronounce this or another form of absolution:
In the name of Jesus I declare to you:
You are forgiven; your sins are gone.
Be strong in the Holy Spirit, and live for God. **Amen.**

A deacon or a reader says:
May Almighty God have mercy on us,
forgive us our sins,
and make us strong in the Holy Spirit to live for God. **Amen.**

In England an authorised form of absolution is used as set out in Common
Worship *pages 135-137.*

Acclamation
Stand
Let us praise God for his mercy
and give thanks to him for his goodness.

Glory to the Father and to the Son, and to the Holy Spirit;
as it was in the beginning, is now, and shall be for ever. Amen.

A song of praise is sung.

The Collect of the day

MINISTRY OF THE WORD

Readings *from the Bible*

These may be followed by a **Bible Responsory**, *a* **Hymn** *or a* **Scripture Song.**
O bless the God of Israel (CH 706) Blessed be the God of Israel (CH 685) or
Tell out my Soul (CH 712; CP 362) or the traditional Canticles Benedictus
or Magnificat *are particularly suitable.*

The Sermon

RESPONDING

Affirmation of Faith
Do you believe and trust in God the Father?
    I believe in God, the Father almighty,
    creator of heaven and earth.

Do you believe in God the Son?
    I believe in Jesus Christ, God's only Son, our Lord.
    who was conceived by the Holy Spirit,
    born of the Virgin Mary,
    suffered under Pontius Pilate,
    was crucified, died, and was buried;
    he descended to the dead.
    On the third day he rose again,
    he ascended into heaven,
    he is seated at the right hand of the Father,
    and he will come again to judge the living and the dead.

Do you believe in God the Holy Spirit?
    I believe in the Holy Spirit
    the holy catholic Church,
    the communion of saints,
    the forgiveness of sins,

> **the resurrection of the body,**
> **and the life everlasting. Amen.**

This is the faith of the Church.
> **This is our faith.**
> **We believe and trust in one God,**
> **Father, Son, and Holy Spirit.**

A hymn may be sung.

Prayers

Intercessions, Petitions and Thanksgivings in the form of bidding, silence and collect type prayer.

A general collect
Heavenly Father,
in darkness and in light, in trouble or in joy,
help us to trust your love, to serve your purpose,
and to praise your name,
through Jesus Christ our Lord. Amen.

Gathering all our prayers and praises into one, we pray as our Saviour Christ has taught us:
> **Our Father....**

A hymn may be sung and when the collection is received this prayer may be said:

Lord Jesus Christ, you emptied yourself, taking the form of a servant.
Through your love, make us servants of one another.

Lord Jesus Christ, for our sake you became poor.
May our lives and gifts enrich the life of your world.

GOING OUT AS GOD'S PEOPLE

Let us say together:
Be with us Lord, as we go out into the world.
May the lips that have sung your praise always speak the truth;
may the ears which have heard your Word
listen only to what is good
and may our lives as well as our worship
be always pleasing in your sight,
for the glory of Jesus Christ our Lord. Amen.

Blessing or The Grace.

The power of God hold and lead us.
His heavenly host be our guard.

4   IN THE EVENING

This form developed from informal services held in a parish outside the City of Cork which was experiencing renewal. Some of the material had been published in **Celebrating Common Prayer.**

GATHERING

Greeting
The light and peace of Jesus Christ be with you
and also with you.

As our evening prayer rises before you, O God,
so may your mercy come down on us to cleanse our hearts
and set us free to sing your praise
now and for ever. **Amen.**

A hymn is sung.

Now, my friends, all that is true, all that is noble,
all that is just and pure, all that is lovable and attractive,
whatever is excellent and admirable,
fill our thoughts with these things:
and the God of peace will be with us. (*Based on Philippians 4:8,9*)

Penitence

Psalm 141:1-4,8

The following refrain is recited here and after each section:
> **Let my prayer rise before you as incense,**
> **the lifting up of my hands as the evening sacrifice.**

O Lord, I call to you; come to me quickly;
hear my voice when I cry to you.

Set a watch before my mouth, O Lord,
and guard the door of my lips.   *Refrain*

Let not my heart incline to any evil thing;
let me not be occupied in wickedness.

But my eyes are turned to you, Lord God,
in you I take refuge; do not leave me defenceless. *Refrain*

The Collect of the day

MINISTRY OF THE WORD

Readings
from the Old and New Testament are each followed by silence.

This prayer may be said after the last reading.
Lord, your word is a lamp for our feet.
In darkness and in light, in trouble or in joy,
help us to trust your love,
to serve your purpose, and to praise your name,
through Jesus Christ our Lord. **Amen.**

Scripture Song.
Metrical versions of Nunc Dimittis *(CH 691; CP 360) or* Cantate Domino
(CH 710) are particularly suitable.

Cantate Domino *(Tune: Beethoven's Ode to Joy.)*
Sing to God new songs of worship –
all his deeds are marvellous;
he has brought salvation to us
with his hand and holy arm:
he has shown to all the nations
righteousness and saving power,
he recalled his truth and mercy
to his people Israel.

Sing to God new songs of worship –
earth has seen his victory;
let the lands of earth be joyful
praising him with thankfulness:
sound upon the harp his praises,
play to him with melody;
let the trumpets sound his triumph,
show your joy to God the king!

Sing to God new songs of worship –
let the sea now make a noise;
all on earth and in the waters
sound your praises to the Lord:
let the hills be joyful together,
let the rivers clap their hands,
for with righteousness and justice
he will come to judge the earth.
 © *Michael Baughen (b. 1930)*

The Sermon

RESPONDING

Affirmation of Faith
Stand

Let us confess our faith in the Son of God:

In the beginning was the Word,
and the Word was with God,
and the Word was God.
Through him all things were made;
without him nothing was made that has been made.
In him was life, and that life was the light of us all.

The Word became flesh
and made his dwelling among us.
We have seen his glory,
the glory of the One and Only Son,
who came from the Father,
full of grace and truth.   *John 1:1,3,4,14*

A hymn may be sung.

Prayers
Kneel

An Evening Litany.

The Taizé Chant, Kyrie eleison, *is particularly suitable sung softly but the response* Lord, have mercy *may be substituted.*

That the rest of this day may be holy, peaceful and full of your presence,
in faith we pray,
Kyrie, kyrie eleison.

That the work we have done and the people we have met today may bring us closer to you,
in faith we pray,
Kyrie, kyrie eleison.

That we may be forgiven our sins and failures,
in faith we pray,
Kyrie, kyrie eleison.

That we may hear and respond to your call to peace and justice,
in faith we pray,
Kyrie, kyrie eleison.

That you will sustain the life and hope of those who are lonely, oppressed and anxious,

in faith we pray,
Kyrie, kyrie eleison.

That you will strengthen us in your service, and fulfil our hearts with longing for your kingdom,
in faith we pray,
Kyrie, kyrie eleison.

Other topics may be freely introduced as desired, and lead in to the response with, 'in faith we pray,'

The litany concludes:
God our Saviour, you know us and love us,
you hear our prayer:
Keep us in the eternal fellowship of Jesus Christ our Lord. Amen.

A general collect
Lighten our darkness, Lord, we pray,
and in your great mercy
defend us from all perils and dangers of this night;
for the love of your only Son, Jesus Christ our Lord. Amen.

Gathering all our prayers and praises into one, we pray as our Saviour Christ has taught us:
Our Father...

GOING OUT AS GOD'S PEOPLE

In peace we will lie down and rest:
For you alone, Lord, make us dwell in safety.

Abide with us, Lord Jesus,
For the night is at hand and the day is now past.

As the night-watch looks for the morning:
So do we long for you, O Christ.

May the risen Lord Jesus watch over us and renew us
as he renews the whole of creation.
May our hearts and lives echo his love. **Amen.**

Let us bless the Lord.
Thanks be to God.

5 WATERFORD Form C

This order is an adaptation of Form C developed in Waterford Cathedral. It is included to show how the basic orders may be locally adapted for regular use; in this case once a month at the Principal Service. It has been re-shaped to conform to the format of this book.

GATHERING

Greeting

This is the day that the Lord has made.
We will rejoice and be glad in it.

The night has passed and the day lies open before us.

The light and peace of the Jesus Christ be with you all
and also with you.

Penitence

The word of God is living and active: it judges the thoughts and intentions of the heart. Therefore, let us cast away the world of darkness and walk in the light of Christ, humbly confessing our sins in penitence and faith.

Kneel

God be gracious to us and bless us,
and make your face shine upon us.
     Lord, have mercy.
     Lord, have mercy.

May your ways be known on earth,
your saving power among the nations.
     Christ, have mercy.
     Christ, have mercy.

You, Lord, have made known your salvation,
and reveal your justice in the sight of the nations.
     Lord, have mercy.
     Lord, have mercy.

The Absolution is pronounced by a priest.

Acclamation

Stand

We stand as forgiven people
therefore let us praise God for his mercy
and give thanks to him for his goodness.

Glory to the Father, and to the Son, and to the Holy Spirit;
as it was in the beginning, is now, and shall be for ever. Amen.

The Spirit of God fills the whole earth:
Come, let us worship.

Song of Praise
All Created things (a metrical version of Benedicite CH 682)

The Collect of the day

MINISTRY OF THE WORD

Readings
Psalm
The Sermon

RESPONDING

Affirmation of Faith
Do you believe and trust in God the Father?
I believe in God, the Father Almighty,
creator of heaven and earth

Do you believe and trust in his Son Jesus Christ?
I believe in Jesus Christ, God's only Son, our Lord,
who redeemed us and all the world.

Do you believe and trust in the Holy Spirit?
I believe in the Holy Spirit
who sanctifies us and all the people of God.

This is the faith of the Church.
This is our faith.
We believe and trust in one God,
Father, Son, and Holy Spirit.

Prayers
The Lord be with you
and also with you.

Let us pray

Prayers as required on the day concluding with **The Lord's Prayer**

A hymn may be sung.

GOING OUT AS GOD'S PEOPLE

Let us say together
Be with us Lord, as we go out into the world.
May the lips that have sung your praise always speak the truth;
may the ears which have heard your Word
listen only to what is good
and may our lives as well as our worship
be always pleasing in your sight,
for the glory of Jesus Christ our Lord. Amen.

Blessing

6 ADVENT

This order has been used on different Sundays in the season with the appropriate prayers for the candle-lighting on the Advent Wreath.

GATHERING

Greeting
From the One who is, and who was, and who is to come, the Almighty:
Grace, light and peace be with you all
and also with you.

Our King and Saviour draws near:
Come, let us worship.

Hymn   Hark the glad sound! the Saviour comes (CH 124; CP 27)

Penitence
When the Lord comes, he will bring to light things now hidden in darkness, and will disclose the purposes of the heart. In that light we confess our sins.

Let us kneel and confess our sins to God our Father.
O God, our Father in heaven,
we confess that we have sinned against you
and against our brothers and sisters.
The things we have said and done have not proclaimed your
reign of truth and love.
Forgive our sins,
and come quickly to save us;
through the coming King, our Saviour Jesus Christ. Amen.

A priest pronounces this absolution
In the advent of Christ the dawn from on high breaks upon us with light and healing.
God looks with favour on you,
and forgives all your sins
In the name of Jesus, receive his pardon,
be strong in the Holy Spirit, and live for God. **Amen**.

Acclamation
Stand
Let us praise God for his mercy
and give thanks to him for his goodness.

Father, we give you thanks and praise
through Jesus Christ your Son, our Lord.

Jesus is Lord of all creation.
O come, let us adore him.

Jesus left the glory of heaven.
O come, let us adore him.

Jesus was born of the Virgin Mary.
O come, let us adore him.

Jesus was cradled in a manger.
O come, let us adore him.

Jesus died to set us free.
O come, let us adore him.

Jesus was raised to life again.
O come, let us adore him.

Jesus reigns in glory now.
O come, let us adore him.

Jesus will come again as judge.
O come, let us adore him.

We worship and adore you with the angels and all the company
of heaven, saying
Holy, holy, holy Lord,
God of power and might,
heaven and earth are full of your glory.
Hosanna in the highest.

THE ADVENT WREATH

Children may be invited to come forward and help to light the Candles – one
on the First Sunday, increasing to four as the season progresses.

We light *this/these* candle(s) as a sign of the coming light of Christ.

Advent means coming. We are preparing ourselves for the coming
of Jesus who was born in Bethlehem and who will come again at
the end of time.

The First Sunday of Advent.

God of Abraham and Sarah,
and of all the patriarchs of old,
you are our Father too.
Your love is revealed to us in Jesus Christ,
Son of God and Son of David.
Help us in preparing to celebrate his birth
to make our hearts ready for your Holy Spirit to make his home
among us.
We ask this through Jesus Christ,
the Light who is coming into the world.

Lord Jesus, Light of the world,
born in David's city of Bethlehem,
born like him to be a king:
Be born in our hearts this Christmastide,
be king of our lives today.

The Second Sunday of Advent.

God our Father,
you spoke to the prophets of old of a Saviour who would bring peace.
You helped them to spread the joyful message of his coming kingdom.
Help us in preparing to celebrate his birth,
to share with those around us the good news of your power and
love.
We ask this through Jesus Christ,
the Light who is coming into the world.

Lord Jesus, Light of the world,
the prophets said you will bring peace
and save your people in trouble.
Give peace in our hearts at Christmastide,
and show all the world God's love. Amen.

The Third Sunday of Advent

God our Father,
you gave to Zechariah and Elizabeth in their old age a son called John.
He grew up strong in spirit,
prepared the people for the coming of the Lord,
and baptized them in the Jordan to wash away their sins.
Help us who have been baptized into Christ,
to be ready to welcome him into our hearts,
and to grow strong in faith by the power of the Spirit.
We ask this through Jesus Christ,
the Light who is coming into the world.

**Lord Jesus, Light of the world,
John told the people to prepare,
for you were very near.
As Christmas grows closer day by day,
help us to be ready to welcome you now.**

The Fourth Sunday of Advent

God our Father,
the angel Gabriel told the Virgin Mary
that she was to be the mother of your son.
Though Mary was afraid, she responded to your call with joy.
Help us, whom you call to serve you,
to be like her in your great work
of bringing to our world your love and healing.
We ask this through Jesus Christ,
the Light who is coming into the world.

**Lord Jesus, Light of the world,
thank you for Gabriel, who brought the Good News,
thank you for Mary, your mother, blessed for ever.
Bless your Church preparing for Christmas;
and bless us your children who long for your coming.**

*If the Advent Wreath ceremony is not used **the Collect of the day** is said.*

THE MINISTRY OF THE WORD

Hymn Our God reigns. (CH 129) or Hills of the North, rejoice (CH 128; CP 29)

Readings

Bible Responsory
Stand

We wait for your loving kindness, O God,
in the midst of your temple.

The glory of the Lord shall be revealed
and all flesh shall see it together.

Show us your mercy, O Lord,
and grant us your salvation.

Scripture Song
Benedictus (*or* Magnificat *on the Fourth Sunday*); *metrical forms may be used.*

The Sermon

RESPONDING

Affirmation of Faith

We say together in faith
Holy, holy, holy is the Lord God almighty,
who was, and is, and is to come.

We believe in God the Father,
who created all things:
for by his will they were created
and have their being.

We believe in God the Son,
who was slain:
for with his blood,
he purchased us for God,
from every tribe and language, from every people and nation.

We believe in God the Holy Spirit:
the Spirit and the Bride say, 'Come!'
Even so come, Lord Jesus! Amen.
(based on Revelation 4:8,11; 5:9; 22:17,20)

Prayers
In joyful expectation of his coming to our aid we pray to Jesus.

As a response to the Hebrew word, *Maranatha*, a New Testament
Advent prayer, we respond with the rest of that prayer: *Amen.*
Come, Lord Jesus.

Maranatha
Amen. Come, Lord Jesus.

Come to your Church as Lord and Judge.
We pray for the Church in ....
and for our parish and congregation..........
Help us to live in the light of your coming
and give us a longing for your Kingdom.

Maranatha:
Amen. Come, Lord Jesus.

Come to your world as King of the nations.
We pray for the leaders of the nations, and their people
for governments and all in positions of authority and responsibility,
especially for ......
For [*UK Elizabeth, our Queen*] / [*RI our President*].

and for *her / our* government
Before you rulers will stand in silence.
>Maranatha:
>**Amen. Come, Lord Jesus.**

Come to your people with a message of victory and peace.
We pray for those who live in fear,
for the sick,
for the bereaved,
for those in dangerous occupations.
Give us victory over death, temptation and fear.
>Maranatha:
>**Amen. Come, Lord Jesus.**

Come to us as Saviour and Comforter.
We pray for strength to follow you as real disciples,
for power to witness when opportunity arises
and for power to love even when we feel unloving.
Break into our lives where we live with failure and distress,
and set us free to serve you for ever.
>Maranatha:
>**Amen. Come, Lord Jesus.**

Come from heaven, Lord Jesus, with power and great glory.
Lift us up to meet you,
that with all your saints and angels and all whom you have
declared righteous in your sight,
we may live and reign with you in your new creation.
>Maranatha:
>**Amen. Come, Lord Jesus.**

All say together:
**Open our eyes to your presence
and awaken our hearts to praise.
To all who long for your Son's return
grant perseverance and patience
that we may announce in word and deed
the good news of the kingdom.
We ask this through him whose coming is certain,
whose day draws near;
your Son, our Lord Jesus Christ,
who lives and reigns with you in the unity of the Holy Spirit
one God, now and for ever. Amen.**

Let us gather up all our prayer and praise and say together the prayer our Saviour Christ has taught us:

Our Father...

Hymn   O come, O come Emmanuel (CH 135; CP 32)).

GOING OUT AS GOD'S PEOPLE

All say together

God be in my head and in my understanding
God be in my eyes and in my looking
God be in my mouth and in my speaking
God be in my heart and in my thinking
God be at my end and at my departing.

Blessing

May God the Father,
judge all merciful,
make us worthy of a place in his kingdom.   **Amen**

May God the Son,
coming among us in power,
reveal in our midst the promise of his glory.   **Amen.**

May God the Holy Spirit
make us steadfast in faith,
joyful in hope and constant in love. **Amen.**

And the blessing of God almighty,
the Father, the Son, and the Holy Spirit, be with you
and remain with you always.   **Amen.**

Go in the peace of Christ
Thanks be to God.

7 CHRISTMAS

GATHERING

Greeting

I bring you good news of great joy:
a Saviour has been born to you. Alleluia!
Unto us a child is born, a son is given. Alleluia!

Hear the words of Saint Luke:
When the angels had left them and gone into heaven, the shepherds said one to another, 'Let us go now to Bethlehem and see this thing that has taken place, which the Lord has made known to us.' So they went with haste, and found Mary and Joseph, and the child lying in a manger.

He is Christ the Lord.
We worship and adore him.

A hymn may be sung.

Penitence

Let us pray.
As we kneel with the shepherds before the newborn Christ child, we open our hearts in penitence and faith:
Christ the light of the world has come to dispel the darkness of our hearts.
In his light let us examine ourselves and confess our sins.

After the words, *We have sinned* the response is, *Forgive - and heal us.*

Silence is kept.

Lord of grace and truth,
we confess our unworthiness to stand in your presence as your children.
> We have sinned:
> **forgive - and heal us.**

The Virgin Mary accepted your call to be the mother of Jesus.
Forgive our disobedience to your will
> We have sinned:
> **forgive - and heal us..**

Your Son our Saviour was born in poverty in a manger.
Forgive our greed and rejection of your ways.
> We have sinned:
> **forgive - and heal us.**

The shepherds left their flocks to go to Bethlehem.
Forgive our self-interest and lack of vision.

> We have sinned:
> **forgive - and heal us.**

The wise men followed the star to find Jesus the king.
Forgive our reluctance to seek you.

> We have sinned:
> **forgive - and heal us.**

> Lord have mercy upon us.
> **Christ have mercy upon us.**
> Lord have mercy upon us.

A priest says
May the God of all healing and forgiveness
draw you to himself
that you may behold the glory of his Son,
the Word made flesh,
and be cleansed from all your sins.
Receive your forgiveness,
through Jesus Christ our Lord.   **Amen.**

Stand
The Collect of the day

MINISTRY OF THE WORD

Readings *appropriate to the season and Christmas carols.*

Benedictus *or* Magnificat *may be sung*

The Sermon

RESPONDING

Affirmation of Faith
Let us confess our faith in the Son of God:

In the beginning was the Word,
and the Word was with God,
and the Word was God.
Through him all things were made;
without him nothing was made that has been made.
In him was life, and that life was the light of us all.

**The Word became flesh
and made his dwelling among us.
We have seen his glory,
the glory of the One and Only Son,
who came from the Father,
full of grace and truth.**

Before the collection the following may be said
You know the grace of our Lord Jesus Christ, that though he was
rich, yet for our sakes he became poor, so that we through his
poverty might become rich.   *2 Corinthians 8:9*

A hymn may be sung during which a collection for charity is taken up.

Prayers

Let us pray

A prayer of thanksgiving
Blessed are you, God of all Glory,
through your son Jesus Christ.
His name is Jesus:
Because he saves his people from their sin.
He is Emmanuel: God with us.
He has come to his people and set them free.
He gave us the glory of heaven: and took the form of a servant.
The Word was made flesh: and we beheld his glory.
In humility he walked the path of obedience: to die on the cross.
God raised him to the highest place above
and gave him the name above every name:
So all in heaven and earth will fall at his feet,
and proclaim to the glory of God:
Jesus Christ is Lord!

To you, O Christ, Word of the Father,
we offer our lowly prayers and sincere thanks;
for love of our human race
you most wonderfully and humbly chose to be made man,
and to take our nature as nevermore to lay it by;
so that we might be born again by your Spirit
and restored in the image of God;
to whom, one blessed Trinity,
be given all honour, might, majesty and power,
now and for ever. **Amen.**

Intercession

Father, at this time your Son our Saviour was born in human
form:
renew your Church as the body of Christ:

> Lord, in your mercy
> **Hear our prayer.**

At this time Christians the world over are celebrating his birth:
open our hearts that he may be born in us today:

> Lord, in your mercy
> **Hear our prayer.**

At this time there was no room for your Son in the inn:
protect with your love those who have no home and all who live
in poverty:

> Lord, in your mercy
> **Hear our prayer.**

At this time Mary in the pain of labour brought your Son to birth:
hold in your hand all who are in pain or distress today.

> Lord, in your mercy
> **Hear our prayer.**

At this time your Christ came as a light shining in the darkness:
bring comfort to all who suffer in the sadness of our world.

> Lord, in your mercy
> **Hear our prayer.**

At this time shepherds in the field heard good tidings of joy:
give us grace to proclaim and witness to the good news of Christ's
redemption.

> Lord, in your mercy
> **Hear our prayer.**

At this time the angels sang 'Peace to God's people on earth':
strengthen those who work for peace and justice in the troubled
and divided world of today.

> Lord, in your mercy
> **Hear our prayer.**

At this time strangers found the Holy Family, and saw the baby
lying in the manger:
bless our homes, the families to which we belong and all whom
we love.

> Lord, in your mercy
> **Hear our prayer.**

At this time heaven is come down to earth, and earth is raised to heaven:
we remember with thanksgiving all those who have gone through death in the hope of heaven and be a comfort to all who have been bereaved in recent days.
> Lord, in your mercy
> **Hear our prayer.**

At this time angels and shepherds worshipped at the manger throne:
receive the worship we offer today in fellowship with the saints and the whole company of heaven.
> Lord, in your mercy
> **Hear our prayer.**

We say together:
Remember, O Lord, what thou hast wrought in us
and not what we deserve
and as thou hast called us to thy service make us worthy of our calling;
through Jesus Christ our Lord. Amen.

Let us gather up all our prayer and praise and say together the prayer our Saviour Christ has taught us:
> **Our Father...**

GOING OUT AS GOD'S PEOPLE

A hymn may be sung.

Blessing
May the eagerness of the shepherds,
the joy of the angels,
the perseverance of the wise men,
the obedience of Joseph and Mary,
and the peace of the Christ-child
be yours this Christmas.
And the blessing of God almighty,
the Father, the Son and the Holy Spirit,
be upon you and remain with you always. **Amen.**

8 THE WEEK OF PRAYER FOR CHRISTIAN UNITY

GATHERING

Greeting
The love of the Lord be with you all
and also with you.

Christ is our peace, who has made us one,
he has broken down the barriers that divided us.   *Ephesians 3: 14*

A hymn may be sung.

Bidding
Jesus prayed, '.... that they may all be one. As you, Father, are in me
and I am in you, may they also be in us, so that the world may
believe.' *John 17: 21*

In the presence of the God and Father of us all,
we meet together *(from our various churches)* aware that this prayer
of Jesus was offered on the night on which he was betrayed.
We give thanks for the spiritual unity
which is already ours as members of the Body of Christ,
but conscious that the Church has betrayed its Lord over the centuries in allowing itself to become divided and that we continue to
accept divisions, saying 'I am of Canterbury' or 'I am of Geneva' or
'I am of Rome' or whatever.
So we shall offer our penitence as well as our praise
and we shall pray for the recovery of the full visible unity of
Christ's Church, for which he prayed and by the means he shall
chose
that with our common life renewed
the world may see the church as a sign of the unity of all
humankind.

Penitence
The Lord is gentle and full of compassion; let us ask forgiveness.

A moment of silence for reflection and self-examination

Lord Jesus, you came to reconcile us to one another and to the
Father.
      Lord, have mercy.
      Lord, have mercy.

Lord Jesus, you heal the wounds of pride and intolerance, of sin
and division.

Christ, have mercy.
Christ, have mercy.

Lord Jesus, you intercede for us with your Father.
Lord, have mercy.
Lord, have mercy.

May almighty God cleanse us from sin
and make us worthy of the kingdom of his glory. **Amen.**

Acclamation

Stand

Lift up your hearts.
We lift them to the Lord.

Let us give thanks to the Lord our God
It is right to give our thanks and praise.

Father, it is our duty and our joy, to give you thanks through Jesus
Christ our Lord:
By him, your only Son, you restored to us peace at the price of his
blood shed on the Cross, reconciling the world to yourself
Glory to you, gracious Father.

By him you have led us to know you,
so that by the bond of one faith and one baptism
we have become his body, with one hope of our calling.
Glory to you, gracious Father.

By him you have given to all peoples your holy Spirit,
who works marvels by innumerable gifts
distributes many and varied graces,
empowers us to proclaim the good news in many languages,
gathers us together in unity,
and fills the entire Church.
Glory to you, gracious Father.

This great company, on earth and in heaven,
one in the Lord Jesus,
joins with angels and archangels in one song of joy:
Holy, Holy, Holy Lord, God of power and might,
heaven and earth are full of your glory.
Hosanna in the highest!

The Collect for Unity *is said.*
Lord Jesus Christ,
who said to your apostles,
Peace I leave with you, my peace I give to you:
look not on our sins but on the faith of your Church,
and grant it the peace and unity of your kingdom;
where you are alive and reign with the Father
and the Holy Spirit, one God, now and for ever. **Amen.**

MINISTRY OF THE WORD

A hymn may be sung.

Readings

The Song of The Church (Te Deum) *may be sung. Metrical form: God we praise you (CH 696, CP 450)*

Bible Responsory

There is one body, one Spirit, one hope in God's call.
One God and Father of all who is over all and in all.

One Lord, one faith, one baptism.
One God and Father of all.

Glory to the Father, and to the Son, and to the Holy Spirit.
There is one body, one Spirit, one hope in God's call.

The Sermon

RESPONDING

Stand

Affirmation of Faith

There is one Lord, one faith and one baptism.
United in Christ, let us confess the faith we hold in common.

All recite the Apostles' Creed together.

A hymn is sung.

Prayers

Kneel

In faith let us pray to God our Father, through his Son Jesus Christ,
in the strength of the Holy Spirit.
Kyrie eleison.

For the Church of God throughout the world, in all its branches and denominations, that all may boldly confess Jesus as Messiah, Lord and Saviour.
Kyrie eleison.

For all who serve the church as leaders, that their confession may be true and their leadership compassionate.
Kyrie eleison.

For the leaders of the nations, that they establish and defend justice and peace, that the wisdom of God may direct their decision-making.
Kyrie eleison.

For those who suffer oppression or violence because of their profession of faith,
Kyrie eleison.

That the churches may discover again their visible unity as the love of Christ draws together all who are baptized in his name.
Kyrie eleison.

That the churches may attain communion in the eucharist around the one table and so truly anticipate on earth the messianic banquet in heaven.
Kyrie eleison.

That the churches may recognise in each other's ministries the one ministry to which they have been appointed by the Holy Spirit.
Kyrie eleison.

That we in the congregations in this neighbourhood may more and more work together that even here people may know that we belong together in the fellowship of the Holy Spirit.
Kyrie eleison.

Eternal God and Father,
whose Son at supper prayed that his disciples might be one,
as he is one with you:
Draw us closer to him,
that in common love and obedience to you
we may be united to one another
in the fellowship of the one Spirit,
that the world may believe that he is Lord,
to your eternal glory;
through Jesus Christ our Lord. **Amen.**

Gathering all our prayers and praises into one, we pray as our Saviour Christ has taught us:
Our Father....

Hymn   The Church's one Foundation (CH 528; CP 585)

GOING OUT AS GOD'S PEOPLE

A prayer of Commitment which may be said by all
God our Father, in the name of Jesus and in the strength of the Holy Spirit,
we commit ourselves to you and to one another,
to live, work and pray as one body in Christ.
[To do apart nothing that we can do together,
and to do together what we cannot do apart.]
Give us vision, give us courage, give us joy
that the world may believe that Jesus is Lord,
to your eternal glory. Amen.

The Peace may be exchanged after this introduction
If there is any encouragement in Christ, any consolation from love, any sharing in the Spirit: be of the same mind, having the same love, being in full accord and of one mind. *Philippians 2:1,2*

The peace of the Lord be always with you
and also with you.

After this there is a time of silent prayer.

Then all present join hands and say together with eyes open,
The grace of our Lord Jesus Christ.
and the love of God,
and the fellowship of the Holy Spirit,
be with us all evermore. Amen.

9 THE PRESENTATION OF CHRIST

At the end of the Epiphany season conscious of the days lengthening the congregations of Lecale Group gathered for a joint service focusing on the Presentation of Christ.

GATHERING

Greeting
Come close to God, and he will come close to you.
The Lord our God is worthy to receive glory and honour and power, for he has redeemed us.

We pray together
Blessed are you, Heavenly Father,
for your have sent us your salvation.
In our worship today inspire us by your Holy Spirit
to see and hear Jesus speaking to us as we listen to your word.
We ask this in his Name. Amen.

Hymn   When morning gilds the skies (CH 344; CP 619)

Penitence
Hear the words of Saint John:
God's love for us was revealed when God sent his only Son into the world so that we could have life through him.   *1 John 4:9*
If we say we have no sin we deceive ourselves, and the truth is not in us.
If we confess our sins, God is faithful and just and will forgive our sins and cleanse us from all unrighteousness.   *1 John 1.8,9*

Trusting in God's mercy and forgiveness, let us kneel and ask for the forgiveness of our sins.

A moment of silence for reflection and self-examination.

Lord Jesus, you came to reconcile us to one another and to the Father.
Lord, have mercy.
Lord, have mercy.

Lord Jesus, you heal the wounds of pride and intolerance.
Christ, have mercy.
Christ, have mercy.

Lord Jesus, you pardon the sinner and welcome the penitent.
Lord, have mercy.
Lord, have mercy.

May almighty God grant us pardon and peace,
strengthen us in faith,
and make us witnesses to his love,
revealed to us in Jesus Christ our Lord. **Amen.**

Acclamation
Stand

From the rising of the sun to its setting
your glory is proclaimed to all the world.

Blessed are you, king of the nations,
to you be praise and glory for ever.

O worship the Lord in the beauty of holiness.
Let the whole earth stand in awe of him.

Father, through the mystery of the Word made flesh
we have seen your salvation:
Christ your Son, presented in the temple,
by your Spirit revealed as the glory of Israel
and the light of the nations.
So with all the angels we give you glory, saying,
Holy, Holy, Holy Lord, God of power and might,
heaven and earth are full of your glory.
Hosanna in the highest!

The Collect of the day is said

MINISTRY OF THE WORD

A hymn is sung: Be still for the presence of the Lord (CH 325; CP 383)

First Reading   1 Samuel 1: 20-end

Psalm 122

Second Reading Luke 2: 22-40

Bible Responsory

The Virgin mother brings Jesus to Jerusalem and presents the
Infant Lord in the Temple of God.
Sun of Righteousness, our God, for ever.

He gives light to those who sit in darkness.
Sun of Righteousness, our God, for ever.

Simeon, in old age, taking him in his arms, rejoices,
for his eyes have seen the Lord's Messiah:
Sun of Righteousness, our God, for ever.

Anna, giving thanks, speaks of him to all
who look for the redemption of Israel:
Sun of Righteousness, our God, for ever.

Christ, faithful over God's house as a son:
Sun of Righteousness, our God, for ever.

From him we may receive mercy and find grace in time of need:
Sun of Righteousness, our God, for ever.

Glory to the Father and to the Son and to the Holy Spirit.
Sun of Righteousness, our God, for ever.

Nunc Dimiitis *is sung or the hymn Faithful vigil ended (CH 691; CP 360)*

The Sermon

RESPONDING

Stand
Affirmation of Faith
The Apostles' Creed *is said*

or
Let us affirm our faith in Jesus Christ the Son of God.
Though he was divine,
he did not cling to equality with God,
but made himself nothing.
Taking the form of a slave,
he was born in human likeness.
He humbled himself
and was obedient to death,
even the death of the cross.
Therefore God has raised him on high,
and given him the name above every name:
that at the name of Jesus
every knee should bow,
and every voice proclaim that Jesus Christ is Lord,
to the glory of God the Father. Amen.
based on Philippians 2: 6-11

A hymn may be sung.

Prayers

Kneel

Let us pray that the radiance of Christ will illumine the church, the nations and all who seek the light.

A moment of silence

We pray for the church:
that, beholding the light revealed to the nations, we may glorify you and reflect the light of your glory to others.

> Lord in your mercy:
> **hear our prayer.**

We pray that the natural resources of your creation, the environment and all living creatures may be preserved from abuse and neglect.

> Lord in your mercy:
> **hear our prayer.**

We pray for those who have no voice in our society, for immigrants and refugees, for those in exile from their own lands or who are being held captive with no access to justice.

> Lord in your mercy:
> **hear our prayer.**

We pray for those who have difficulties in their relationships with others, for those who fight addictions to alcohol, drugs or gambling; for all who are sick in body or mind and need your healing strength.

> Lord in your mercy:
> **hear our prayer.**

We pray for the aged among us, that like Anna and Simeon their voices may be strong in witness to Christ and that from them all may receive encouragement in their own pilgrimage through life.

> Lord in your mercy:
> **hear our prayer.**

We remember those your servants who have gone from us in peace, praying that with them we may at length fully see your salvation in that place where sorrow and pain are no more.

> Lord in your mercy:
> **hear our prayer.**

All say together
Hear our spoken and silent prayers, O God of light,
and reveal yourself to us more fully each day;
through Jesus Christ our Lord Amen.

Gathering all our prayers and praises into one, we pray as our
Saviour Christ has taught us:
Our Father....

GOING OUT AS GOD'S PEOPLE

Hymn   Be thou my vision, O Lord of my heart (CH 643; CP 386)

The Blessing

Christ, the Son of God, born of Mary,
fill you with his grace to trust his promises and obey his will;
and the blessing of God almighty,
the Father, the Son and the Holy Spirit,
be with you and remain with you always. **Amen.**

All turn to face the door
To a troubled world
Peace from Christ

To a searching world
Love from Christ

To a dying world
Hope from Christ.

Amen.

10 MOTHERING SUNDAY

This service was prepared by members of the Liturgical Advisory Committee as one of a projected series for special occasions. It was approved by the House of Bishops and eventually published on the Church of Ireland website. The original has been adapted to the Service of the Word format for this book.

GATHERING

Greeting

The Lord be with you
and also with you.

Sentence

As a mother comforts a child so will I comfort you, says the Lord.
Isaiah 66:13

Introduction

For many years the Fourth Sunday in Lent has been observed as Mothering Sunday. The tradition arose from a sentence in St Paul's Letter to the Galatians, which for many centuries was read in the Epistle of this Sunday: in it St Paul writes of 'Jerusalem which is above is free, which is the mother of us all'. So, on this day we give thanks to God who gives us New Birth, and for the Church which, like a mother, nurtures us in the life of the Spirit. We also give thanks for our own human mothers, and for all the qualities of mothering, given and received in this congregation.

A hymn may be sung.

Penitence

Let us confess our sins to God our Father.
**Almighty and merciful God
we have sinned against you,
in thought, word and deed.
We have not loved you with all our heart.
We have not loved others as our Saviour Christ loves us.
We are truly sorry.
In your mercy forgive what we have been,
help us to amend what we are,
and direct what we shall be;
that we may delight in your will
and walk in your ways;
through Jesus Christ our Saviour. Amen.**

A priest says
Through the Cross of Christ,
may God have mercy on you,
pardon you, and set you free.
Know that you are forgiven — and be at peace.
May God strengthen you in all goodness,
and keep you in life eternal. **Amen.**
[*In England an authorised absolution must be used.*]

Acclamation
Stand
O Lord, open our lips
and our mouth will proclaim your praise.

O God, make speed to save us.
O Lord, make haste to help us.

Glory to the Father, and to the Son, and to the Holy Spirit;
as it was in the beginning, is now, and shall be for ever. Amen.

The Collect of Mothering Sunday
God of compassion,
whose Son Jesus Christ, the child of Mary,
shared the life of a home in Nazareth,
and on the cross drew the whole human family to himself
Strengthen us in our daily living
that in joy and in sorrow
we may know the power of your presence
to bind together and to heal;
through Jesus Christ our Lord. **Amen.**

MINISTRY OF THE WORD

Praise the Lord.
The Lord's name be praised.

Psalm
Psalm 27: 1-6 or 34 or 84 or 87 or 122 or 139: 1-18

Readings

Old Testament   1 Samuel 1: 20-28 or Proverbs 4: 1-9 or Proverbs 31: 10-31 or Micah 4: 1-5

New Testament   Ephesians 5: 22 - 6: 4 or Colossians 3: 12-17 or 2 Timothy 1: 3-10

Gospel   Matthew 12: 46-50 or Matthew 23: 37-39 or Mark 10: 13-16 or Luke 2: 41-45 or John 19: 23-27

Scripture Song

THE SONG OF OUR ADOPTION   *Ephesians 1: 3-6*

1   Blessèd are you, God and Father of our Lord ˈ Jesus ˈ Christ |
    you have blessed us in Christ with every spiritual ˈblessing •
    in the ˈheaven • ly ˈ realms.

2   Even before the world was made you chose us to be ˈ yours in
    ˈ Christ |
    that we should be holy and ˈ blameless ˈ in your ˈsight.

3   In love you destined us for adoption as your children ˈ through
    Christ ˈ Jesus |
    such was your ˈ pleasure ˈ and your ˈpurpose,

4   to the praise of your ˈ glori•ous ˈ grace |
    which you have freely given us in ˈ your beˈloved ˈ Son.
    Glory to the Father, and ˈ to the ˈ Son |
    and ˈ to the ˈ Holy ˈSpirit.
    As it was in the be ginning • is ˈ now |
    and shall be for ˈ ever.ˈ Aˈmen.

or The SONG OF HANNAH   *1 Samuel 2: 1-4,7,8*
   These words may be used as a refrain
   My heart exults in the Lord: my strength is exalted in my God.

1   My heart exˈults • in the ˈ Lord |
    my strength is exˈalted ˈin my ˈGod.

2   There is none holy ˈ like the ˈ Lord |
    there is none beside you, ˈ no rockˈ like our ˈ God.   *Refrain*

3   For you O Lord are a ˈ God of ˈ knowledge |
    and by | you our | actions • are ˈ weighed.

4   The bows of the ˈ mighty • are ˈbroken |
    but the ˈ feeble ˈ gird on ˈ strength.   *Refrain*

5   You Lord make ˈ poor • and make ˈ rich |
    you bring ˈ low • and you ˈalso • eˈxalt.

6   You raise up the ˈ poor • from the ˈ dust |
    and lift the ˈ needy ˈ from the ˈash-heap.   *Refrain*

7   You make them ˈ sit with ˈ princes |
    and inˈherit • a seat of ˈ honour.

8   For yours O Lord are the ˈ pillars • of the ˈ earth |
    and on them ˈ you have ˈ set the ˈ world.   *Refrain*
    Glory to the Father, and ˈ to the ˈ Son |
    and ˈ to the ˈ Holy ˈSpirit.
    As it was in the be ginning • is ˈ now |
    and shall be for ˈ ever.ˈ Aˈmen.

or a metrical version of Magnificat (CH 712; CP 362)

The Sermon

RESPONDING

The Apostles' Creed is said.

A symbolic act like children presenting flowers to mothers and other adult women in the congregation, drama or mime may be included at some stage. But care needs to be taken that minority groups are not ignored e.g. single people, those unable to have children, adopted children and orphans.

A hymn may be sung.

Prayers

These may include some of the following:

THANKSGIVINGS

We thank God for giving us others to share in our lives:

For parents, and the love which brought us to birth:
> We praise you, O Lord;
> **and bring you thanks today.**

For mothers who have cherished and nurtured us:
> We praise you, O Lord;
> **and bring you thanks today.**

For fathers who have loved and supported us,
> We praise you, O Lord;
> **and bring you thanks today.**

For brothers and sisters with whom we have shared our home:
> We praise you, O Lord;
> **and bring you thanks today.**

For children and their parents:
> We praise you, O Lord;
> **and bring you thanks today.**

For other relatives and friends, who have been with us in our hopes and joys and times of sadness:
> We praise you, O Lord;
> **and bring you thanks today.**

For all who first spoke to us of Jesus, and have drawn is into the family of our Father in heaven:
> We praise you, O Lord;
> **and bring you thanks today.**

**Help us to live
as those who belong to one another,
and to you, our Father, now and always. Amen.**

or

**Almighty God,
we praise you for the blessings brought to the world through
your Church.
We bless you for the grace of the sacraments,
for our fellowship in Christ with you and with each other,
for the teaching of the Scriptures, and for the preaching of your word.
We thank you for the holy example of your saints,
for your faithful servants departed this life,
and for the memory and example of all that has been true and
good in their lives.
Number us with them in the company of the redeemed in heaven;
through Jesus Christ our Lord. Amen.**

Intercessions

For mothers

Lord Jesus, you know well the blessing an earthly home can bring:
Receive our thanks for all the love we have received in our homes,
especially from those who have nurtured us from our earliest years.
Hear our prayers for mothers everywhere,
that they may never lose heart nor ever be taken for granted,
but receive from their children the honour and love you showed
to your mother, Mary,
even as you were suffering on the Cross.
Bless and keep them all, for your love's sake. **Amen**

For those in need

Remember, O Lord, all those in need:
people with no good food or proper clothes,
no home of their own, or no work to do;
those who have neither family nor friends
and no knowledge of your love.
Supply their needs.
Bless those who try to help them
and bring us all to trust in you.
We ask this is Jesus' name. **Amen**.

For those who live alone

God our Father,
we ask you to bless all who live alone,
those who have lost their partner in marriage,

those who have never married,
those whose families are grown up and away from home
and those who have outlived other members of their families
and many of their friends:
Be with them to assure them of your love
and of their value to you every moment of their lives,
and enable them to rejoice in the fellowship of your Church
on earth and in heaven;
through Jesus Christ our Lord. **Amen.**

A prayer which may be said by children together.or repeated phrase by phrase after a Sunday school teacher or other person.

Father in heaven,
bless all mothers
and those who look after us in our daily lives.
Make us grateful for their goodness
and thankful for their care.
Help us to respond to them in loving obedience;
following the example of Jesus, your Son, our Lord. Amen.

Gathering all our prayers and praise into one, let us pray the
prayer of God's family, as our Saviour Jesus Christ has taught us,
and say:
    Our Father ....

GOING OUT AS GOD'S PEOPLE

A hymn is sung.

Blessing

May the Lord who brought us to birth by his Spirit,
strengthen us for the Christian life. **Amen.**

May the Lord who provides for all our needs
sustain us day by day. **Amen.**

May the Lord whose steadfast love is constant as a mother's care,
send us out to live and work for others. **Amen.**

And the blessing of God Almighty.
the Father, the Son, and the Holy Spirit,
be with you and remain with you always. **Amen.**

11 PALM SUNDAY – Celebrating the Passion

This order was developed over a number of years in the Lecale group of parishes, people from all the member churches coming together as an all-age congregation. The children distributed the palm branches as the congregation gathered and led the clergy from the door to the sanctuary during the singing of the first hymn. The service was designed to focus on the Passion of Jesus. The same set of familiar hymns was used each year between the readings which varied according to the year in the Revised Common Lectionary. The meditation that replaced the sermon was always short and led into a time of penitence. The use of the 'traditional' Good Friday prayers was a later addition and helped to round off an order to which people looked forward each year.

GATHERING

Palm Crosses are distributed to members of the congregation.

Greeting
The Lord be with you
and also with you

Prayer
Assist us mercifully with your Holy Spirit, good Lord,
that we may enter upon our meditation of those mighty acts,
by which you have wrought our redemption;
through Jesus Christ our Lord. **Amen.**

All say together

**Lord Jesus, we hold in our hands these palm crosses,
symbols both of your royal entry to Jerusalem
and of your precious death for our redemption:
During this Holy Week may they be a constant reminder to us of your love
that may we draw closer to you each day:
for you died and are alive,
King for ever,
reigning with the Father in the unity of the Holy Spirit. Amen.**

COMMEMORATING THE ENTRY INTO JERUSALEM

All face the Church door
Hosanna, to the Son of David!
Hosanna in the Highest!

Psalm 24 verses 7 to 10 are sung

7   Lift up your heads, O gates; be lifted up, you ever│lasting │ doors; │
    and the King of │ glory │ shall come │ in.

8   'Who is the │ King of │ glory?' │
    'The Lord, strong and mighty, the │ Lord • who is │ mighty
    in │ battle.'

9   Lift up your heads, O gates; be lifted up, you ever│lasting │ doors; │
    and the King of │ glory │ shall come │ in.

10 'Who is this │ King of │ glory?' │
    'The Lord of hosts, │ he is the │ King of │ glory.'

The Gospel

Hear the Gospel of our Saviour Christ according to Saint Matthew
/ Mark / Luke

Glory to you, Lord Jesus Christ.

Year A   Matthew 21: 1-11   Year B   Mark 11: 1-11   Year C   Luke 19: 28-40

This is the Gospel of the Lord.
Praise to you, Lord Jesus Christ.

This prayer is said
Almighty God,
your Son Jesus Christ was hailed as King on the Sunday before he died;
Grant that as we honour him in prayer and praise,
so we may always seek your glory by obedience to your will;
through Jesus Christ our Lord,
who is alive and reigning with you and the Holy Spirit,
one God, now and for ever. **Amen.**

Hosanna, to the Son of David!
Hosanna in the Highest.

*All turn, holding up the palm crosses, and sing the hymn 'All glory, laud,
and honour' (CH 217; CP 128)*

MINISTRY OF THE WORD

Readings from The Passion of our Saviour Christ
No words are used before or after any reading

THE SUPPER
Year A   Matthew 26: 17-30
Year B   Mark 14: 17-26
Year C   Luke 22: 14-23, 31-34

Hymn   An upper room did our Lord prepare (CH 399; CP 130)

THE BETRAYAL

Year A   Matthew 26: 30-56
Year B   Mark 14: 32-50
Year C   Luke 22: 39-53

Hymn   *There is a green hill far away, (CH 244; CP 123)*

THE DENIAL

Year A   Matthew: 26: 69-75
Year B   Mark 53-54, 66-72
Year C   Luke 22: 54-61

Hymn   *Great God, your love has called us here (CH 416, CP 133)*

THE CONDEMNATION

Year A   Matthew: 27: 1-2, 11-26
Year B   Mark 15: 1-15
Year C   Luke 23: 1-4, 13-25

Hymn   *Glory be to Jesus (CH 220; CP 108)*

THE CRUCIFIXION   *Congregation standing*

Year A   Matthew: 27: 32-50, 54
Year B   Mark 15: 22-39
Year C   Luke 23: 26, 32-47

Meditation

RESPONDING

Penitence

The form penitence takes is at the service leader's choice.
The penitential kyries for Passiontide may be used.

Lord God,
you sent your Son to reconcile us to yourself and to one another.
> Lord, have mercy.
> **Lord, have mercy.**

Lord Jesus,
you heal the wounds of sin and division.
> Christ, have mercy.
> **Christ, have mercy.**

Holy Spirit,
through you we put to death the sins of the body – and live.
> Lord, have mercy.
> **Lord, have mercy.**

or these prayers may be said:

Make our hearts clean, O God;
and renew a right spirit within us.

Father eternal, giver of light and grace,
we have sinned against you and against our neighbour,
in what we have thought, in what we have said and done,
through ignorance, through weakness,
through our own deliberate fault.
We have wounded your love, and marred your image in us.
We are sorry and ashamed, and repent of all our sins.
For the sake of your Son Jesus Christ, who died for us,
forgive us all that is past;
and lead us out from darkness to walk as children of light. Amen.

This prayer is said:
God our Father,
the strength of all who put their trust in you,
mercifully accept our prayers;
and because, in our weakness,
we can do nothing good without you,
grant us the help of your grace,
that in keeping your commandments
we may please you, both in will and deed;
through Jesus Christ our Lord. **Amen.**

or a priest pronounces the absolution.
Almighty God,
who forgives all who truly repent,
have mercy upon you
pardon and deliver you from all your sins,
confirm and strengthen you in all goodness
and keep you in life eternal;
through Jesus Christ our Lord. Amen.

Hymn   The Servant King (CH 219; CP 432)

Prayers

God sent his Son into the world, not to condemn the world, but
that through him the world might be saved, that all who believe
in him might be delivered from the power of sin and death and
become heirs with him of eternal life.
Therefore we pray to our heavenly Father for people everywhere
according to their needs.

Let us pray for the one holy catholic and apostolic Church of God
throughout the world —

for unity in faith, in witness and in service
for all church leaders and ministers,
and the people whom they serve,
for our bishop, and the people of this diocese
for this *parish*,
for all Christians in this community
that God will confirm his Church in faith, increase it in love, and preserve it in peace.

Silence

Eternal God,
by your Spirit the whole body of your faithful people
is governed and sanctified:
Receive our prayers which we offer before you
for all members of your holy church,
that in our vocation and ministry
we may truly and devoutly serve you;
through our Lord and Saviour Jesus Christ. **Amen**.

Let us pray for all nations and peoples of the world, and their leaders —
[*UK for Elizabeth our Queen and her government,*]
[*RI   for our President and our government*]
for all elected to represent the people in [*UK parliament, assembly*] [*RI the oireachtas*] and council
for those who administer the law and all who serve in public office
for all who strive for justice and reconciliation,
that by God's help they may seek justice and truth that the world may live in peace and freedom.

Silence

Most gracious God and Father,
in whose will is our peace:
Turn our hearts and the hearts of all to yourself,
that by the power of your Spirit
the peace which is founded on justice
may be established throughout the world;
through Jesus Christ our Lord. **Amen.**

Let us pray for all who suffer and are afflicted in body or in mind:
for the hungry and homeless,
the destitute and the oppressed,
and all who suffer persecution, doubt, and despair,
for the sorrowful and bereaved,

for prisoners and captives
and those in mortal danger,
that God will comfort and relieve them, and grant them the
knowledge of his love,
and that he will stir up in us the will and patience to minister to
their needs.

Silence

Gracious God,
the comfort of all who sorrow,
the strength of all who suffer,
hear the cry of those in misery and need.
In their afflictions show them your mercy,
and give us, we pray, the strength to serve them,
for the sake of him who suffered for us,
your Son Jesus Christ our Lord. **Amen.**

Let us pray for those who do not believe the Gospel of Christ —
for those who follow other faiths and creeds
for those who have not heard the message of salvation
for all who have lost faith
for the contemptuous and scornful
for those who are enemies of Christ and persecute those
who follow him
for all who deny the faith of Christ crucified
that God will open their hearts to the truth and lead them to faith
and obedience.

Silence

Merciful God,
creator of the peoples of the earth and lover of souls,
have compassion on all who do not know you
as you are revealed in your son Jesus Christ.
Let your Gospel be preached with grace and power
to those who have not heard it.
Turn the hearts of those who resist it,
and bring home to your fold those who have gone astray;
that there may be one flock under one Shepherd,
Jesus Christ our Lord. **Amen**.

Let us commit ourselves to God,
and pray for the grace of a holy life,
that with all who have departed this life and have died in the
peace of Christ,
and with those whose faith is known to God alone,

we may be accounted worthy to enter into the fullness of the joy
of our Lord,
and receive the crown of life in the day of resurrection.
Silence

Eternal God of unchanging power and light,
look with mercy on your whole church.
Bring to completion your saving work,
so that the whole world may see the fallen lifted up,
the old made new,
and all things brought to perfection
by him through whom all things were made,
our Lord Jesus Christ,
who lives and reigns with you,
in the unity of the Holy Spirit,
one God, for ever and ever.   **Amen**.

Finally, let us pray for all those things for which our Lord would
have us ask and gather all our prayers in the words our Saviour
taught us:
> **Our Father, ...**

GOING OUT AS GOD'S PEOPLE

Hymn   Ride on, ride on in majesty (CH 238; CP 129)

Blessing
Christ crucified draw you to himself
and grant that you find in his cross
a sure ground for faith, a firm support for hope,
and the assurance of sins forgiven:
and the blessing of God Almighty,
the Father, the Son and the Holy Spirit,
be with you and remain with you always. **Amen.**

12 EASTERTIDE

This order was developed for a Sunday in the season of Eastertide and includes an opportunity for people to re-affirm their baptismal commitment while not being a full renewal of vows. Readings may be those of the Sunday. Other readings may be chosen.

GATHERING

The grace of our Lord Jesus Christ and the love of God and the fellowship of the Holy Spirit be with you
and also with you.

Blessed are you, Sovereign God, overflowing in love.
Your Holy Spirit hovered over the unformed world,
overshadowed Mary when the Word took flesh,
and made ready the cleansing sacrifice of Calvary.
Blessed are you, Sovereign God, overflowing in love.

On the first Easter Day you raised your Son,
triumphant over sin, death and evil.
He showed himself alive to his friends
and before ascending to your side commissioned them
to proclaim the Gospel to all the world,
and to make disciples, baptizing them in your holy Name.
Blessed are you, Sovereign God, overflowing in love.

With the harvest of Pentecost has dawned the age of the Spirit.
Now the flame of heaven rests on every believer;
praises burst from the lips of people of all nations,
strong and weak, women and men tell out your word;
the young receive visions, the old receive dreams.
Blessed are you, Sovereign God, overflowing in love.

With the new wine of the Spirit
your people proclaim the majesty of your love.
Amid the birth pains of the new creation
the way of light is made known.
Blessed are you, Sovereign God, overflowing in love.

Source of freedom, giver of life,
blessed are you, Sovereign God, Light of the world. Amen.

Hymn   Jesus lives, thy terrors now   (CH 272; CP 148)

Penitence

Christ our passover lamb has been offered for us.
Let us then rejoice by putting away all malice and evil, confessing
our sins with a sincere and true heart.

O Jesus Christ, risen master and triumphant Lord,
we come to you in sorrow for our sins,
and confess to you our weakness and unbelief.

We have lived by our own strength,
and not by the power of your resurrection.
>> In your mercy, forgive us.
>> **Lord, hear us and help us.**

We have lived by the light of our own eyes,
as faithless and not believing.
>> In your mercy, forgive us.
>> **Lord, hear us and help us.**

We have lived for this world alone,
and doubted our home in heaven.
>> In your mercy, forgive us.
>> **Lord, hear us and help us.**

A priest pronounces this absolution
God who is both power and love,
forgive you and free you from your sins,
heal and strengthen you by his Spirit,
and raise you to new life in Christ our Lord. **Amen.**

A hymn is sung.

Acclamation

Lift up your hearts.
We lift them to the Lord.

Let us give thanks to the Lord our God.
It is right to give our thanks and praise.

We give you thanks and praise
for the gospel we have received.
Christ died for our sins: Alleluia!
He is risen indeed. Alleluia!

Death comes to all through Adam,
and sin reigns for a time.
New life without end comes through Christ,
and he reigns for ever: Alleluia!

He is risen indeed. Alleluia!

Death, where is your victory?
Death, where is your sting?
Death is swallowed up in victory -
the victory you give us in Christ: Alleluia!
He is risen indeed. Alleluia!

We have been crucified with Christ,
and live his risen life,
to praise you for ever with angels and archangels:
Holy, holy, holy Lord,
God of power and might,
heaven and earth are full of your glory.
Hosanna in the highest.

The Collect of the day

MINISTRY OF THE WORD

Reading   Acts 4: 32 -35

Scripture Song A SONG OF PETER

Refrain: **Praise be to the God and Father of our Lord Jesus Christ.**

1 Praise be to the God and Father of our Lord Jesus Christ:
   who in his great mercy gave us new birth as his children.

                                                    Refrain

2 He has raised Jesus Christ from the dead:
   so that we have a sure hope in him.   *Refrain*

3 We have the promise of an inheritance that can never be spoilt:
   because it is kept for us in heaven.   *Refrain*

4 The ransom that was paid to free us:
   was not paid in silver or gold;   *Refrain*

5 but in the precious blood of Christ:
   the Lamb without spot or stain.   *Refrain*

6 God raised him from the dead and gave him glory:
   so that we would have faith and hope in God.   *Refrain*

Glory to the Father, and to the Son, and to the Holy Spirit;
as it was in the beginning, is now, and shall be for ever. Amen.

Reading   John 20: 19-31

Hymn   *Ye choirs of new Jerusalem, (CH 292; CP 162)*

The Sermon

RESPONDING

Affirmation of Faith
Let us declare our faith in the resurrection of our Lord Jesus Christ:
Christ died for our sins
in accordance with the scriptures;
he was buried;
he was raised to life on the third day
in accordance with the scriptures;
afterwards he appeared to his followers,
and to all the apostles:
this we have received,
and this we believe. Amen.   *1 Corinthians 15: 3-7*

Declaration of commitment
Will you continue in the apostles' teaching and fellowship,
in the breaking of bread, and in the prayers?
   With the help of God, I will.

Will you persevere in resisting evil, and, whenever you fall into
sin, repent and return to the Lord?
   With the help of God, I will.

Will you proclaim by word and example the good news of God in
Christ?
   With the help of God, I will.

Will you seek and serve Christ in all people, loving your neighbour as yourself?
   With the help of God, I will.

Will you acknowledge Christ's authority over human society, by
prayer for the world and its leaders, by defending the weak, and
by seeking peace and justice?
   With the help of God, I will.

Hymn   The day of Resurrection!   (CH 283; CP 157)

Prayers
We pray to Jesus who is present with us to eternity, saying,
   Jesus, Lord of life,
   in your mercy, hear us.

Jesus, light of the world,
bring the light and peace of your gospel to the nations ...
    Jesus, Lord of life,
    in your mercy, hear us.

Jesus, bread of life,
give food to the hungry
and nourish us all with your word.
    Jesus, Lord of life,
    in your mercy, hear us.

Jesus, way, truth and life for humankind,
be with us and all who follow you in the way,
deepen our appreciation of your truth, and fill us with your life.
    Jesus, Lord of life,
    in your mercy, hear us.

Jesus, Good Shepherd who gave your life for the sheep,
recover the straggler, bind up the injured,
heal and strengthen those who are sick
and enable those who are healthy and strong to work and to play.
    Jesus, Lord of life,
    in your mercy, hear us.

Jesus, the resurrection and the life,
we give you thanks for all who have lived and believed in you...
raise us with them to eternal life.
    Jesus, Lord of life,
    in your mercy, hear us,
    accept our prayers, and be with us always. Amen.

Gathering all our prayers and praises into one, we say as our
Risen Lord has taught us,
    Our Father .....

Hymn   *Thine be the glory, risen, conquering Son (CH 288; CP 160)*

GOING OUT AS GOD'S PEOPLE

Blessing

God the Father,
by whose love Christ was raised from the dead,
open to you who believe the gates of everlasting life. **Amen.**

God the Son,
who in bursting from the grave has won a glorious victory,
give you joy as you share the Easter faith. **Amen.**

God the Holy Spirit,
whom the risen Lord breathed into his disciples,
empower you and fill you with Christ's peace. **Amen.**

And the blessing of God Almighty, the Father, the Son, and the
Holy Spirit, be with you and remain with you always. **Amen.. . .**

Hymn   *Christ triumphant, ever reigning (CH 259; CP 398)*

Go, in the strength of the victory of Christ, to love and serve the Lord.
Thanks be to God. Alleluia! Alleluia!

13 PENTECOST

This order is developed from one used at a Group Service in June - not originally on the Day of Pentecost when the Eucharist is celebrated in all churches of the Group.

GATHERING

Greeting
The Spirit of the Lord be always with you
and also with you.

The Lord is my strength and my song:
and he has become my salvation   *Isaiah 12:2*

Sing to the Lord, for he has done gloriously:
Let this be known in all the earth.   *Isaiah 12:5*

Hymn   Come Down, O Love divine (CH 294; CP 175)

Penitence
As we recall our disobedience to God's commandments and our failure to do his will; let us kneel and confess our sins to God our Father:

Faithful God,
we confess that we have been unfaithful.
We have sinned in thought and word and deed,
We have tried to live by our own strength
and we have failed miserably.
We are truly sorry.
Have mercy on us,
forgive us our sins
and restore us to the joy of your salvation.
For the sake of your Son, Jesus Christ our Lord. Amen.

A priest pronounces this absolution.
Christ died to sin once for all,
and now, victorious lives to God.
Our Saviour has delivered us from the power of darkness
and welcomed us into the realm of light:
For his sake, God grant you pardon and peace
and the remission of all your sins. **Amen.**

Acclamation

Stand

We were washed,
we were sanctified

We were justified,
in the name of Jesus Christ.

Through the Spirit of our God
poured out upon his church.
May glory, honour, praise and dominion
ascend from God's people on earth:
Alleluia, alleluia, alleluia.

A hymn is sung.

The Collect of the day is said.

MINISTRY OF THE WORD

Readings *from the Old and New Testaments, each followed by a short time of silence.*

Psalm 25
Refrain: **Show me your ways O Lord: and teach me your paths.**

1 To you, O Lord, I lift up my soul;
      O my God, in ' you I ' trust; |
    let me not be put to shame;
        let not my ' enemies ' triumph ' over me. *Refrain*

2 Let none who look to you be ' put to ' shame, |
    but let the ' treacherous be ' shamed and frus'trated.

3 Make me to know your ' ways, O ' Lord, |
    and ' teach me ' your ' paths.   *Refrain*

4 Lead me in your ' truth and ' teach me, |
      for you are the God of my salvation;
    for you have I ' hoped ' all the day ' long.

5 Remember, Lord, your com'passion and ' love, |
    for they ' are from ' ever'lasting.   *Refrain*

6 Remember not the sins of my youth or ' my trans'gressions, |
    but think on me in your goodness, O Lord,
        according | to your ' steadfast ' love.   *Refrain*

7 Gracious and upright ' is the 'Lord; |
    therefore shall he teach ' sinners ' in the ' way.

8 He will guide the humble in ⏐doing ⏐right ⏐
  and⏐ teach his ⏐ way to the ⏐ lowly.   *Refrain*

9 All the paths of the Lord are⏐ mercy and ⏐ truth ⏐
  to those who keep his ⏐ covenant⏐ and his ⏐ testimonies.   *Refrain*
  Glory to the Father, and ⏐ to the ⏐ Son ⏐
  and ⏐ to the ⏐ Holy ⏐ Spirit.
  As it was in the be ginning · is ⏐ now ⏐
  and shall be for⏐ ever.⏐ A⏐men.

Scripture Song
a version of Jubilate Deo *(Tune: Darwall's 148th)*
All nations of the world
Be joyful in the Lord:
With willing hands your Master serve
With one accord:
In ceaseless praise
with heart and voice
In him rejoice
through all your days.

Be sure the Lord is God,
Creation's Source and Spring:
In him alone we live, to him
Our lives we bring.
From days of old
He feeds his flock
And guides the wanderers
To his fold.

In gladness go your way:
Approach his courts with song
In thankfulness to him to whom
All things belong.
His name adore
His gracious mercy
Truth and love
For evermore.
© *Edwin Le Grice*

The Sermon

RESPONDING

Stand

Affirmation of Faith

Do you believe and trust in God the Father,
creator of heaven and earth?
I believe and trust in him.

Do you believe and trust in God's Son Jesus Christ,
who redeemed mankind?
I believe and trust in him.

Do you believe and trust in the Holy Spirit
who gives life to the people of God?
I believe and trust in him.

This is the faith of the Church.
This is our faith.
We believe and trust in one God,
Father, Son, and Holy Spirit.

A hymn may be sung.

Prayers

Rejoicing in the resurrection of Jesus we remember in prayer
the church, the world and those in need:

Come, Holy Spirit, bestowed on the church at Pentecost.
Inspire your Church today to be prophetic,
to witness to the Gospel,
and to serve the world.
Give it new visions and power to work to achieve.
That the world may believe.

> For this we pray:
> **Hear us, living God.**

Come, Holy Spirit, to all the nations of the world.
Bring your peace to our conflicts.
Inspire leaders and people to find peace
and let justice take its place in all human affairs.
That all God's children may live.

> For this we pray:
> **Hear us, living God.**

Come, Holy Spirit, bring healing to those in need,
comfort to those who grieve
and courage to those without hope.
That all may be renewed.

For this we pray:
Hear us, living God.

Come, Holy Spirit, to this congregation,
may we become peacemakers and reconcilers,
as and when you give us opportunity.
That our common life may reveal your love.
For this we pray:
Hear us, living God.

Come, Holy Spirit, and at the last bring us
with all who have loved the Lord Jesus in life and are now at rest
to the fulfilment of the kingdom.
For this we pray:
Hear us, living God.

Heavenly Father,
with alleluias in our hearts and on our lips,
we commend to your care all for whom we pray,
trusting in your mercy, through Jesus Christ our Lord.. **Amen.**

Gathering our prayers into one, we pray as our Lord himself has
taught us,
Our Father...

GOING OUT AS GOD'S PEOPLE

A hymn is sung.

Blessing

Go, and know that the Lord goes with you:
let him lead you each day into the quiet place of your heart,
where he will speak with you;
know that he loves you and watches over you -
that he listens to you in gentle understanding,
that he is with you always,
wherever you are and however you may feel.

The Spirit of truth lead you into all truth,
give you grace to confess that Jesus Christ is Lord,
and to proclaim the words and works of God:
and the blessing of God almighty,
the Father, the Son and the Holy Spirit
be with you and remain with you always. **Amen.**

Go, with the inner empowering of the Holy Spirit, to love and
serve the Lord.
Thanks be to God.

14 TRINITY SUNDAY

GATHERING

Greeting
The Lord be with you
and also with you.

Holy, holy, holy is the Lord God Almighty,
who was, and is, and is to come!

Penitence
Kneel
Holy, holy, holy.
When our eyes have seen the Lord of hosts we echo the words of
Isaiah, 'Woe is me! I am lost.'
We long for the fire of God's cleansing to touch our unclean lips,
for our iniquity to be removed and our sins wiped out.
So let us kneel before God, Three in One and One in Three, the
Father, Son and Holy Spirit with confession on our lips.

Holy, holy, holy is the Lord of hosts; the whole earth is full of his glory:
Father, you come to meet us when we return to you.
> Lord, have mercy.
> **Lord, have mercy.**

Woe is me, for I am lost; I am a person of unclean lips.
Jesus, you died on the cross for our sins.
> Christ, have mercy.
> **Christ, have mercy.**

Your guilt is taken away, and your sin forgiven.
Holy Spirit, you give us life and peace.
> Lord, have mercy.
> **Lord, have mercy.**

A priest stands and says
Almighty God have mercy on you, forgive you all your sins
through our Lord Jesus Christ, strengthen you in all goodness,
and by the power of the Holy Spirit keep you in eternal life. **Amen.**

Acclamation

Blessed be God: Father, Son, and Holy Spirit
and blessèd be his kingdom, now and for ever. Amen.
O Blessèd Trinity,
in whom we know the Maker of all things, seen and unseen,
the Saviour of all both near and far:

By your Spirit enable us so to worship your divine Majesty,
that with all the company of heaven, we may magnify your glorious name, saying:

**Holy, Holy, Holy Lord, God of power and might,
heaven and earth are full of your glory.
Hosanna in the highest!**

Hymn   Immortal, invisible, God only wise (CH 6; CP 474)

The Collect of the day
Almighty and everlasting God,
you have given us your servants grace,
by the confession of a true faith,
to acknowledge the glory of the eternal Trinity
and in the power of the divine majesty to worship the Unity:
Keep us steadfast in this faith,
that we may evermore be defended from all adversities;
for you live and reign, one God, for ever and ever. **Amen.**

THE MINISTRY OF THE WORD

Psalm 150
1 Alleluia.
     O praise God ˈ in his ˈ holiness; |
   praise him in the ˈ firmament ˈof his ˈ power.
2 Praise him for his ˈ mighty ˈ acts; |
   praise him acˈcording to his ˈ excellent ˈ greatness.
3 Praise him with the ˈ blast of the ˈ trumpet; |
   praise him upˈon the ˈ harp and ˈ lyre.
4 Praise him with ˈ timbrel and ˈ dances; |
   praise him upˈon the ˈ strings and ˈ pipe.
5 Praise him with ˈ ringing ˈcymbals; |
   praise him upˈon the ˈ clashing ˈ cymbals.
6 Let everything ˈ that has ˈ breath |
   praise the ˈ Lord. ˈAlleˈluia
   Glory to the Father, and ˈ to the ˈ Son |
   and ˈ to the ˈ Holy ˈ Spirit.
   As it was in the be ginning • is ˈ now |
   and shall be forˈ ever.ˈ Aˈmen.

Old Testament Reading   *Isaiah 6: 1-8*

Hymn   Bright the vision that delighted (CH 316; CP 392)

New Testament Reading   *John 14: 8-17*

Scripture Song   *Great and Wonderful*   (*Tune : Nicea*)
Wonderful your deeds, Lord God the Almighty:
Just and true, great King of all the world, are all your ways.
Only you are holy, in thankful adoration
Your name, O Lord, with joy your people praise.

Nations of the world shall worship in your presence.
The justice of your dealings your glory here displays.
To the one who reigns in majesty and glory
And to the Lamb be everlasting praise.
© *1994   Edwin le Grice*

The Sermon

RESPONDING

Affirmation of Faith
Stand

Do you believe and trust in God the Father, creator of heaven and
earth?
>   **I believe and trust in him.**

Do you believe in God the Son, who redeemed the world?
>   **I believe and trust in him.**

Do you believe in God the Holy Spirit, who gives life to the people of God?
>   **I believe and trust in him.**

This is the faith of the Church.
>   **This is our faith.**
>   **We believe and trust in one God,**
>   **Father, Son, and Holy Spirit.**

or
The Catholic Faith is this:
that we worship one God in Trinity,
and Trinity in Unity.
>   **Glory to the Father, and to the Son, and to the Holy Spirit;**
>   **as it was in the beginning, is now, shall be for ever. Amen.**

Hymn   *O worship the King* (*CH 34; CP 546*)

Prayers

Let us pray:

We come boldly to the throne of grace,
praying to the almighty God, Father, Son and Holy Spirit for
mercy and grace, saying
> **We plead before your throne in heaven.**

Father of heaven, whose love profound
a ransom for our souls has found:
We pray for the world, created by your love,
for its nations and governments...
> Extend to them your peace, pardoning love, mercy and grace.
> **We plead before your throne in heaven.**

Almighty Son, incarnate Word,
our Prophet, Priest, Redeemer, Lord:
We pray for the Church, created for your glory,
for its ministry to reflect those works of yours...
> Extend to us your salvation, growth, mercy and grace.
> **We plead before your throne in heaven.**

Eternal Spirit, by whose breath
the soul is raised from sin and death:
We pray for families and individuals, created in your image,
for the lonely, the bereaved, the sick and the dying...
> Breathe on them the breath of life
> and bring them to your mercy and grace.
> **We plead before your throne in heaven.**

Mysterious Godhead, three in one,
Thrice holy - Father, Spirit, Son:
We pray for ourselves,
for your church, for all whom we remember before you...
Bring us all to bow before your throne in heaven,
> Grant us life and pardon, mercy and grace for all eternity.
> **We plead before your throne in heaven.**

A general collect
Almighty God,
may we worship you with lips and lives
proclaiming your majesty
and finally see you in your eternal glory:
Holy and Eternal Trinity,
one God, now and for ever. Amen.

Let us sum up all our prayers and praises in the words our Saviour Christ has taught us, saying :

Our Father....

Hymn   *God / Thou whose almighty word (CH 324; CP 267)*

GOING OUT AS GOD'S PEOPLE

Let us kneel, and say together:
Be with us Lord, as we go out into the world.
May the lips that have sung your praise
always speak the truth;
may the ears which have heard your Word
listen only to what is good
and may our lives as well as our worship
be always pleasing in your sight,
for the glory of Jesus Christ our Lord. Amen

Blessing

God the Father,
who first loved us and made us accepted in the beloved Son,
bless you. **Amen.**

God the Son,
who loved us and washed us from our sins in his own blood,
bless you. **Amen.**

God the Holy Spirit,
who sheds abroad the love of God in our hearts,
bless you. **Amen.**

The blessing of the one true God,
to whom be all love and all glory for time and for eternity,
come down upon you and remain with you always. **Amen.**

The Lord be with you
and also with you.

The Lord give us his peace
and life eternal. Amen.

15 THE BIRTH OF SAINT JOHN THE BAPTIST

In the parishes of Lecale group it was customary at the end of the Sunday School year to hold a family service. This often fell on or about the festival of the Birth of Saint John the Baptist. This form was used on one such occasion. On others children and young people contributed their own music and composed their own prayers of thanksgiving and intercession. The structure enabled the service to have meaning for those of all ages.

GATHERING

This is the day which the Lord has made.
Let us be glad and rejoice in it.

Loving God, we have come to worship you.
Help us to remember that you are here with us.
May we pray to you in faith
sing your praise with gratitude
and listen to your words with eagerness;
through Jesus Christ our Lord. Amen.

The Lord is my strength and my song:
He has become my salvation.

Sing to the Lord, for he has done great things.
Let this be known in all the world.

Hymn   Morning has broken (CH 58; CP 260)

Penitence

Let us kneel and recall our foolish disobedience to God's commandments and our failure to do his will; remembering that in Jesus God has come to his people and set them free:

For our foolishness.
and our thoughtless use of the gifts of God's creation.
          Lord, have mercy.
          Lord, have mercy.

For our failure to heed his teaching
and our failure to love as he has loved us.
          Christ, have mercy.
          Christ, have mercy.

For our selfishness, our carelessness in worship
and for ignoring the Holy Spirit's prompting.

Lord, have mercy.
Lord, have mercy.

God of truth and love
be merciful to us
as we claim your promise of forgiveness
through Jesus Christ our Lord.

God, who is faithful and just,
assure you* of pardon and peace.
Thanks be to God.
* *A deacon or reader says 'us'*

Acclamation

Stand

Give praise to God almighty:
It is right to give our thanks and praise.

It is indeed right and fitting, our duty and our joy,
always, here and everywhere, to give you thanks,
Lord, holy Father, almighty and eternal God,
and on this midsummer day,
the birthday of Saint John the Baptist
to praise you for the wonders of your power.

Before he was conceived you gave him his name,
signifying that he is your gift :
before he was born you filled him with the Holy Spirit:
on his birthday you loosed the tongue of his father
to sing and prophesy to your praise and glory.

Christ the Lord knew him as the Forerunner
and among all those born of women he counted him the greatest.

And so, for all the gifts
with which you endowed this the last of the ancient prophets,
we join with all the powers of heaven in their joyful hymn of
praise, saying:

Holy, holy, holy Lord,
God of power and might,
heaven and earth are full of your glory.
Hosanna in the highest.

The Collect
Almighty God,
by whose providence your servant John the Baptist
was wonderfully born,
and sent to prepare the way of your Son our Saviour,
by the preaching of repentance:
Lead us to repent according to his preaching,
and, after his example, constantly to speak the truth,
boldly to rebuke vice, and patiently to suffer for the truth's sake;
through Jesus Christ our Lord. **Amen.**

MINISTRY OF THE WORD

Old Testament Reading *1 Kings 19: 1-18*

Psalm 34
as in the hymn Through all the changing scenes of life (CH 114; CP 604)

Gospel Reading   *Luke 1: 57-66*

Scripture Song
O bless the God of Israel CH 706
or (Tune: Nun Danket)
We bless the Lord our God
For this, his visitation:
To David's house he came
To bring us liberation.
As prophets had declared
From foes he set us free
To serve him without fear
In holy liberty.

Prophet of God most high -
This, child, is your vocation:
Before Christ's face to spread
The knowledge of salvation:
Hope of forgiveness bring
Through his redeeming love,
Who scatters death's dark cloud.
Our Dayspring from Above!

Birth of Saint John the Baptist

The Father now we bless
Who kept his holy promise
To faithful Abraham,
And showered his love upon us:
Through Christ the promised King
On whom the Spirit came.
The praise of Three in One
We evermore proclaim.
© *Edwin Le Grice*

The Sermon

RESPONDING

Affirmation of Faith
Do you believe and trust in God the Father,
creator of heaven and earth?
> **I believe and trust in him.**

Do you believe and trust in God's Son Jesus Christ
who redeemed mankind?
> **I believe and trust in him.**

Do you believe and trust in the Holy Spirit
who gives life to the people of God?
> **I believe and trust in him.**

This is the faith of the Church.
> **This is our faith.**
> **We believe and trust in one God,**
> **Father, Son, and Holy Spirit.**

Hymn   God has spoken to his people, alleluia! (CH 380)

Prayers
Just and holy God,
you have promised that you will come near to us when we come
near to you:

Cleanse our hands and purify our hearts as we bow before you
and bring before you the needs of our world, saying
> Lord, in your mercy:
> **hear our prayer.**

We pray for one another when like John our faith is tested...
In our pain, give us perseverance.
In our ignorance, wisdom.

In our doubt, faith.
>Lord, in your mercy:
>**hear our prayer.**

We pray for our families, neighbours and friends...
In our life together, give us love and honesty.
Take away envy, ambition and disorder,
and make us peacemakers, full of peace and integrity.
>Lord, in your mercy:
>**hear our prayer.**

We pray for those in need, inside and outside the Church...
We pray for justice in our society,
for forgiveness for our favouritism,
and for the insight to love those who are rich in faith
yet poor in the eyes of the world.
>Lord, in your mercy:
>**hear our prayer.**

We pray for our government and for the leaders of the nations...
And for all who direct the daily affairs of our community,
our public representatives (*UK in parliament and council*)
(*RI in the oireachtas and local councils*).
Set a guard over their words
and show them better ways to resolve differences than
confrontation and name-calling.
>Lord, in your mercy:
>**hear our prayer.**

We pray in faith for those who are sick and in trouble...
And for all in the healing professions
that they may be hands to convey your healing.
We commend all who today dwell in darkness and in the shadow
of death,
for the bereaved and all who grieve.
>Lord, in your mercy:
>**hear our prayer.**

We rejoice in our fellowship with all the prophets of old like Amos
and Elijah who strove to turn people back to you, with John the
Baptist and all the saints of the Kingdom,
Together with all who hunger and thirst to see right prevail, bring
us to inherit the kingdom you promise those who love you.
>Lord in your mercy:
>**hear our prayer.**

**Lord, God of Israel and our God also,
as we celebrate the birth of John the Baptist
challenge us to turn to you again.
May the Christ to whom he pointed,
comfort us with his salvation
that we may live lives that are holy and righteous all our days.
These our prayers we bring to you through Jesus Christ our
Lord. Amen.**

Gathering all our prayers and praises together in the words our
Saviour Christ has taught us we delight to say:

> **Our Father....**

Hymn   Sing to God new songs of worship   (CH 710 and above page 20)

GOING OUT AS GOD'S PEOPLE

We say together,
**Creator God,
we rejoice in the different seasons.
As the summer sun shines may we know the warmth of your
love.
As the rains fall may we rejoice in the softness of your care.
As the winds blow may we be strengthened by your Holy Spirit.
So may we live each day to your glory,
through Jesus Christ our Lord. Amen.**

Blessing
May the love of the Cross,
the power of the Resurrection,
and the presence of living Lord
be with you always. **Amen.**

And the blessing of the eternal God:
Creator and Father
Risen Lord and Saviour,
Giver of holiness and love,
be with you all, now and for ever. **Amen.**

16 HARVEST THANKSGIVING

Many people prefer a 'traditional' service of Morning or Evening Prayer or a Eucharist for Harvest Thanksgiving. However, Service of the Word offers many possibilities. Everything included here has been used but the thanksgiving in Gathering and the intercessions in Responding have never been used at the same service. If children are bringing gifts it makes sense for the thanksgiving prayers to be linked to that event and individual children might read the prayers provided they can be heard!

GATHERING

An Introit may be sung by a choir (congregation remain seated) or the hymn, For the beauty of the earth (CH 350; CP 253) may be sung

Greeting

This is the day that the Lord has made.
Let us rejoice and be glad in it.

The land has yielded its harvest:
God, our God, has blessed us.

God has blessed us:
Let everyone everywhere honour him! Amen.

Hymn   Come ye thankful people come (CH 37; CP 270)
Children may bring appropriate gifts forward.

Thanksgiving

We thank God for the world he has made,
and for all his love and care.

For the warmth of the sun,
        Father in heaven:
        we give you thanks and praise.

For the rain which makes things grow,
        Father in heaven:
        we give you thanks and praise.

For the woods and the fields,
        Father in heaven:
        we give you thanks and praise.

For the sea and the sky,
        Father in heaven:
        we give you thanks and praise.

For the flowers and the animals,
> Father in heaven:
> **we give you thanks and praise.**

For the work of farmers, fisherfolk and gardeners all over the world
by which we have food to eat and enjoy.
> Father in heaven:
> **we give you thanks and praise.**

For all your gifts, and especially for the gift of Jesus to be our Saviour..
> Father in heaven:
> **we give you thanks and praise. Amen.**

Penitence

Let us confess our own sins and the sins of our society in the mis-use of God's creation.

God our Father, we are sorry for the times when we have used
your gifts carelessly and acted ungratefully.
> Lord, hear our prayer, and in your mercy
> **forgive us and help us**

We admit that while we enjoy the fruits of the harvest
we sometimes forget that you have given them to us.
> Lord, hear our prayer, and in your mercy
> **forgive us and help us**

We belong to a nation that is full and satisfied
but we often ignore the cry of the hungry
> Lord, hear our prayer, and in your mercy
> **forgive us and help us**

We are thoughtless and do not care enough for the world that
you have made.
> Lord, hear our prayer, and in your mercy
> **forgive us and help us**

We store up goods for ourselves alone,
and often act as if there was no God, or no heaven.
> Lord, hear our prayer, and in your mercy
> **forgive us and help us**

Heavenly Father we confess these sins and in all our misdoings
> Lord, hear our prayer, and in your mercy
> **forgive us and help us**

**May the God of love bring us back to himself, forgive our sins,
restore us in his image and grant us the assurance of eternal life
in Jesus Christ our Lord. Amen.**

Acclamation

Blessed is the Lord,
for he has heard the voice of our prayer.

Therefore shall our hearts dance within us
and in our song we will praise the Lord.

**Glory to the Father and to the Son, and to the Holy Spirit;
as it was in the beginning, is now, and shall be for ever. Amen**

Song of praise *Jubilate ev'rybody (CH 701)*

The Collect for Harvest Thanksgiving
Almighty and everlasting God,
you have given us the fruits of the earth in their season:
Teach us to remember
that we do not live by bread alone,
and grant us to feed on him
who is the true bread from heaven,
Jesus Christ our Lord,
to whom, with you and the Holy Spirit,
be all honour and glory for evermore. **Amen.**

MINISTRY OF THE WORD

Psalm and Readings *as appointed in the Table of Readings on page 69 of the Church of Ireland Book of Common Prayer.*

Scripture Song *All created things (CH 682) or All creatures of our God and King (CH 24: CP 250)*

The Sermon

RESPONDING

Affirmation of Faith
Let us declare our faith in God

**We believe in God the Father
from whom every family in heaven and on earth is named.**

**We believe in God the Son
who lives in our hearts through faith and fills us with his love.**

**We believe in God the Holy Spirit
who strengthens us with power from on high.**

**We believe in one God
Father, Son and Holy Spirit. Amen.**

A hymn may be sung.

Prayers

Let us pray to God, the Lord of the Harvest, that he will bring to
fruition all that he desires for his creation, saying:

> Father, Lord of creation:
> **in your mercy, hear us.**

Lord of the Harvest,
when we lift up our eyes to perceive with Christ's eyes,
we see that the fields of the world are already white for harvest.
We pray for your Church,
that it may be spiritually equipped to reap the harvest of souls.

> Father, Lord of creation:
> **in your mercy, hear us.**

Lord of the Harvest,
the harvest is plentiful and the labourers are few,
but you make your Church fruitful with many ministries.
We pray for our parish,
that we may grasp the opportunities of the present time.

> Father, Lord of creation:
> **in your mercy, hear us.**

Lord of the Harvest,
you have created the universe by your eternal Word,
and have blessed humankind in making us stewards of the earth.
We pray for your world,
that we may share and conserve its resources,
and live in reverence for the creation
and in harmony with one another.

> Father, Lord of creation:
> **in your mercy, hear us.**

Lord of the Harvest,
whose Son has promised that the Spirit will lead us into all truth,
We pray for the community in which you have set us,
for one another and for ourselves,
that we may bear the harvest of the Spirit
in love and joy and peace.

> Father, Lord of creation:
> **in your mercy, hear us.**

Lord of the Harvest,
though you have given the human race a rich land,

a land of streams and springs, wheat and barley,
vines and oil and honey,
we have made by sin a world of suffering and sorrow.
We pray for those who bear the weight of affliction,
that they may come to share the life of wholeness and plenty.
Father, Lord of creation:
in your mercy, hear us.

Lord of the Harvest,
your Christ, the first-fruits of the resurrection,
will put in the sickle for the harvest of the dead at the end of time.
We pray that we may rejoice
with all who have died in the faith of Christ,
as he brings safely home all whom you have given him
and gathers us all to share together in the banquet of the age to come.
Father, Lord of creation:
in your mercy, hear us.

Creator God,
you give seed for us to sow,
and bread for us to eat;
Make us thankful for what we have received;
make us able to do those generous things
which supply your people's needs;
so all the world may give you thanks and glory. **Amen.**

Gathering all our prayers and thanksgivings in one, we pray as one family,
Our Father...

Hymn   We plough the fields and scatter (CH 47; CP 275)

GOING OUT AS GOD'S PEOPLE

Blessing

May God the Father of our Lord Jesus Christ,
who is the source of all goodness and growth,
pour his blessing upon all things created,
and upon you his children,
that you may use them to his glory and the welfare of all peoples.
and the blessing of God almighty,
the Father, the Son and the Holy Spirit,
be with you and remain with you always. **Amen.**

17 ALL SAINTS

The Litany of the Holy Ones of God, adapted from **Promise of His Glory,** *around which this service was constructed stimulated much interest in the Communion of Saints. The list was read but not printed out. At the end of the service the version of Saint Patrick's Breastplate was used as a re-dedication of our lives in God's service.*

GATHERING

Greeting
The Love of the Lord be always with you
and also with you.

Rejoice, people of God, praise the Lord.
Let us celebrate with joy.
Rejoice in the working of the Holy Spirit
in the lives of men and women.
In their victory the angels rejoice and praise God.

Hymn   Immortal, invisible, God only wise (CH 6; CP 474)

Penitence
Christ calls us to share the heavenly banquet of his love with all the saints in earth and heaven. Knowing our unworthiness and sin, let us ask from God both mercy and forgiveness.

Lord, you are gracious and compassionate.
>Lord, have mercy.
>**Lord, have mercy.**

You are loving to all
and your mercy is over all your creation.
>Christ, have mercy.
>**Christ, have mercy.**

Your faithful servants bless your name
and speak of the glory of your kingdom.
>Lord, have mercy.
>**Lord, have mercy.**

This absolution may be said by a priest
May God our Father forgive you your sins
and bring you to the eternal joy of his kingdom,
where dust and ashes have no dominion. **Amen.**

Acclamation

Stand

Blessed are you, Sovereign God, our light and our salvation,
to you be glory and praise for ever.
Surrounded by a great cloud of witnesses
and glorified in the assembly of your saints
we give you thanks and praise.
With your holy Church in heaven and earth
we acclaim you,
Father, Son and Holy Spirit.
Blessed be God for ever.

The Collect of the day

Almighty God,
you have knit together your elect
in one communion and fellowship
in the mystical body of your Son Christ our Lord:
Grant us grace so to follow your blessed saints
in all virtuous and godly living
that we may come to those inexpressible joys
that you have prepared for those who truly love you;
through Jesus Christ our Lord. **Amen.**

MINISTRY OF THE WORD

First Reading

Psalm 149: 1-5 or Hymn O praise ye the Lord (CH 708; CP 543))

Second Reading.

Scripture Song *a version of* Glory and Honour *(Tune: St Ambrose)*
Glory, honour, endless praises
here we offer, King of kings.
You are source of all our being,
Lord of all created things.

Glory, honour, endless praises
for you, the Lamb for us were slain:
by your blood you ransomed sinners,
set your people free again.

Called to serve from every nation.
Kings and priests, we praise you, Lord
To whom with Father and the Spirit
Lift we our hearts with one accord.
© *Edwin Le Grice*

The Sermon

RESPONDING

Stand
Affirmation of Faith

Let us declare our faith in God.

We believe in God the Father
from whom every family in heaven and on earth is named.

We believe in God the Son
who lives in our hearts through faith and fills us with his love.

We believe in God the Holy Spirit
who strengthens us with power from on high.

We believe in one God
Father, Son and Holy Spirit. Amen.

Hymn   God we praise you, God we bless you. (CH 696; CP 450)

Prayers

A Thanksgiving for the Holy Ones of God

This versicle and response is said after each part

We bless you, O God
and magnify your glorious Name.

For Abraham and Sarah, our ancestors in faith,
journeying into the unknown, yet trusting God's promises:

For Jacob, deceitful younger brother, yet chosen by God,
father of those called by no virtue of their own:

For Moses the lawgiver and Aaron the priest,
who led the people of Israel to freedom and the promised land:

For Esther and Deborah, saviours of their nation,
and for all who act courageously at God's call:

For Elijah, Isaiah, John the Baptist and all the prophets,
who spoke your truth whatever the cost:

For Mary the Virgin, highly favoured One,
called to be Mother of the Lord:

For Andrew and John, the first disciples,
who left all to follow Jesus:

For Mary Magdalene, Salome and Mary, first witnesses of the Resurrection,
and for all who bear witness to Christ:

For Peter and Paul, and all the apostles,
who preached the gospel to Jew and Gentile:

For the writers of the gospels,
and for all who bring the faith of Christ alive for each generation:

For Stephen and Alban, and the noble army of martyrs,
who have faced death for love of Christ:

For Patrick and Columba, for Aidan and Columbanus,
and for all who have carried the gospel to this and other lands:

For Aelred and Bernard,
and for all who live and teach the love of God:

For Anselm and Richard Hooker,
and for all who reveal to us the depths of God's wisdom:

For Benedict and Francis, for Brigid and Bede,
and for all who deepen our common life in Christ:

For Julian of Norwich and Teresa of Avila,
and all who renew our vision of the mystery of God:

For Thomas Cranmer, and all who reform the Church of God,
for Thomas More, and all who stand for integrity in discipleship:

For Gregory and Dunstan, George Herbert, John Keble and Cecil
Frances Alexander,
and all who praise God in poetry and song

For Lancelot Andrews, Jeremy Taylor, John Wesley and Charles Simeon,
and for all who preach the word of God:

For William Wilberforce and Josephine Butler,
and for all who work to transform society:

For Monica, and Mary Sumner,
and for all who nurture faith in home and family:

For Dietrich Bonhoeffer, Oliver Romero and Janani Luwum;
and for all the martyrs and peacemakers of our own time,
who shine as lights in the darkness:

For all the unsung heroes of the faith,
whose names are known to God alone:

The commemorations end
For all those in our own lives who have brought us to this time
and place and who have shown to us the way of holiness:

>Let us honour them with thankful hearts:
>**And glorify God in whom they put their trust.**

A general collect

Almighty and eternal God,
you have kindled the flame of love in the hearts of the saints:
Grant to us the same faith and power of love,
that, as we rejoice in their triumphs,
we may be sustained by their example and fellowship;
through Jesus Christ our Lord. **Amen.**

Let us sum up our prayers and praises in the words our Saviour
Christ has taught us and say:
  Our Father....

Hymn (A version of Saint Patrick's Breastplate, Tune: Bunessan)

1 This day God gives me
Strength of high heaven,
Sun and moon shining,
Flame in my hearth,
Flashing of lightning
Wind in its swiftness,
Deeps of the ocean
Firmness of earth.

2 This day God sends me
Strength as my guardian,
Might to uphold me,
Wisdom as guide.
Your eyes are watchful,
Your ears are list'ning,
Your lips are speaking,
Friend at my side.

3 God's way is my way,
God's shield is round me,
God's host defends me,
Saving from ill.
Angels from heaven,
Drive from me always.
All that would harm me
Stand by me still..

4 Rising I thank you
Mighty and Strong One.
King of creation,
Giver of rest,

Firmly confessing
Threeness of persons.
Oneness of Godhead,
Trinity blest.
© *James Quinn 1968*

GOING OUT AS GOD'S PEOPLE

We say together
Grant, O Lord, that as we leave your house
we may not leave your presence:
be ever near us and keep us close to you,
now and for ever. Amen.

Blessing

May God,
who kindled the fire of his love in the hearts of the saints,
pour upon you the riches of his grace. **Amen.**

May he give you joy in their fellowship
and a share in their praises. **Amen**

May he strengthen you to follow them in the way of holiness
and to come to the full radiance of glory. **Amen**

and the blessing...
Amen

Hymn   For all thy saints, O Lord, (CH 461) or For all the saints, who from
their labours rest (CH 459)

The Lord be with you
and also with you.

Let us bless the Lord.
Thanks be to God.

18 REMEMBRANCE DAY

The Lecale parishes included Down Cathedral in Downpatrick and Remembrance Sunday included laying wreaths on the Cathedral War Memorial. This order of service includes some material from services commended by the archbishops of Canterbury and York and in Northern Ireland by the archbishop of Armagh. The lead in this service was taken by the Precentor of the Cathedral, at that time myself. The order was adapted for country parishes some of which had unique ceremonies like laying a wreath on the grave of an unknown Royal Marine whose body was washed up on the coast in 1917.

GATHERING

Greeting

Grace to you and peace from God our Father and the Lord Jesus Christ.
Thanks be to God.

Hymn   All people that on earth do dwell (CH 683; CP 369)

Bidding

The Precentor says

I bid you welcome to this Cathedral Church as we gather once again for our Remembrance Day service.
We are here to worship God, whose purposes are good;
whose power sustains the world he has made;
who loves us, though we have failed in his service;
who gave Jesus Christ for the life of the world;
who by his Spirit leads us in his way.

As we give thanks for his great works we shall pray for all who suffer through war and the violence of evil men
we shall ask for God's protection for the members of the security forces in this province
for help and blessing that we may do his will
and that the whole world may acknowledge him as Lord and King.

ACT OF REMEMBRANCE

A wreath is placed on the War Memorial.

The Precentor says

Let us remember before God with thanksgiving those who in two world wars and in subsequent conflicts
gave their lives in defence of freedom and justice,
those from this town and county whose memorials are in this

Cathedral Church
and all those known to us.

One who served in the Second World War says
They shall grow not old as we that are left grow old.
Age shall not weary them, nor the years condemn.
At the going down of the sun, and in the morning,
We will remember them
We will remember them.

The Silence

Prayer
Almighty and eternal God,
from whose love in Christ we cannot be parted, either by death or life:
Hear our praise and thanksgiving for all whom we remember this day,
and bring us all, with them, to the fulness of your unending joy;
through Jesus Christ our Lord. **Amen**

MINISTRY OF THE WORD

*Psalm 46   God is our refuge and strength: a very present help in trouble.
or Hymn   God is our strength and refuge (CH 12; CP 443) Tune:
Dambusters March*

Reading   *Isaiah 10: 33 - 11:9*

*Hymn   We turn to Christ anew (CH 604) or Make me a channel of your
peace (CH 503; CP 519)*

Reading   *John 15: 9 -17*

The Sermon

RESPONDING

Penitence
Let us kneel and join in an act of penitence for our sins and for
our share in the sins of the world.
After each petition the response to the words, *Lord, have mercy*, is
Christ, have mercy.
Father eternal, giver of light and grace:
We have sinned against you and against our neighbour,
in what we have thought,
in what we have said,
and in both what we have done and in what we have failed to do:
          Lord, have mercy.
          Christ, have mercy.

We have been deaf to your call to serve as Christ served us.
We have not been true to the mind of Christ.
We have grieved your Holy Spirit.

> Lord, have mercy.
> **Christ, have mercy.**

We confess to you, Lord God, the pride, hypocrisy and impatience of our lives.

> Lord, have mercy.
> **Christ, have mercy.**

We confess our greed, our self-indulgence and our misuse of your gifts to us.

> Lord, have mercy.
> **Christ, have mercy.**

We confess our envy of others, our selfish anger,
our unloving thoughts and actions to our family, friends and neighbours.

> Lord, have mercy.
> **Christ, have mercy.**

We have wounded your love and marred your image in us.
We are sorry and ashamed.

> Lord, have mercy.
> **Christ, have mercy**

Accept our repentance, Good Lord, for the wrongs we have done,
for our blindness to human need and suffering
and for our indifference to injustice and cruelty.

> Lord, have mercy.
> **Christ, have mercy.**

Accept our repentance, Good Lord;
Forgive us our sins of negligence and ignorance as well as our deliberate sins.
Grant us the grace of your Holy Spirit
and time to amend our lives according to your Holy Word.

> Lord, have mercy.
> **Christ, have mercy.**

The priest pronounces this absolution.
Almighty God, who forgives all who truly repent,
Have mercy on you, pardon and deliver you from all your sins,
confirm and strengthen you in all goodness,
and keep you in eternal life;
through Jesus Christ our Lord. **Amen.**

Hymn: Lord, for the years (CH 81; CP 81)

Thanksgiving and intercession

Let us bring our petitions, intercessions and thanksgivings before God.

Heavenly Father, we give you thanks for the wonder of creation,
for the gifts of human life
and for the blessing of human fellowship;
for Christ, your living Word, through whom we are taught the
perfect way of life and the royalty of service,
and for your Spirit who offers his gifts to us for the common good
Lord in your mercy:
Hear our prayer.

For [*UK Elizabeth our Queen , for the Royal Family*:]
For the nations of the world and their governments;
for those called to lead them through the crises of our times,
and through racial and social tensions:
Lord in your mercy:
Hear our prayer.

For the nations which have great powers at their command;
that they may only use such power for the blessing of others and
not for destruction
Lord in your mercy:
Hear our prayer.

For those who share the prophet's vision of swords becoming
ploughshares and spears pruning hooks;
that they may work for the disarming of the nations;
Lord in your mercy:
Hear our prayer.

For all who suffer as a result of war or civil strife;
for the maimed in mind and body;
for those who cannot take part in family life or enjoy the circle of
normal human friendships:
Lord in your mercy:
Hear our prayer.

For the Royal British Legion and for the work of other organizations
of men and women, dedicated to the relief of suffering caused by
war and violence
Lord in your mercy:
Hear our prayer.

For those who seek to make peace and to bring reconciliation
where there is prejudice and hatred, bitterness and division;
especially in this province:

Lord in your mercy:
Hear our prayer.

For your Church's ministry of the Gospel,
that it may proclaim clearly your message of love and peace:

Lord in your mercy:
Hear our prayer.

That men and women everywhere may be able to live in the
freedom and fellowship of your kingdom:

Lord in your mercy:
Hear our prayer.

Almighty God,
who called your church to witness that you were in Christ
reconciling the world to yourself:
Help us to proclaim the good news of your love,
that all who hear it may be reconciled to you;
through him who died and rose again
and reigns with you and the Holy Spirit,
one God, now and for ever. **Amen.**

Almighty God,
our heavenly Father, in whose hands are the living and the dead:
We give you thanks this day
for all those who have laid down their lives
in the service of their country and for justice and freedom.
Grant that the good work which you began in them
may be perfected;
through Jesus Christ our Lord. **Amen.**

Gathering up all our prayer and praise into one, as our Saviour
Christ has taught us, we are bold to say,

Our Father...

Hymn   Thy hand, O God, has guided (CH 529; CP 606)

GOING OUT AS GOD'S PEOPLE

We say together
Almighty God:
We pledge ourselves anew to be peacemakers
in our homes
in our community
in our country
and throughout the world.

Lord God,
Guide us by your Spirit
Give us wisdom
Give us courage
Give us hope
and keep us faithful, now and always. Amen.

To the king of Ages, immortal invisible, the only God,
be honour and glory for ever and ever. **Amen.**

[UK The National Anthem may be sung]

Blessing
God grant to the living, grace
to the departed, rest,
to the Church and to the nations, peace and concord;
and the blessing...

19   CHRIST THE KING

GATHERING

Greeting
This is the day that the Lord has made:
We will rejoice and be glad in it.

Lord, direct our thoughts,
help us to pray,
and lift up our hearts to worship you in Spirit and in truth;
through Jesus Christ our Lord. Amen.

The kingdoms of this world have become the kingdom of our
Lord and of his Christ,
and he shall reign for ever.
Come, let us worship.

Hymn   Seek ye first the kingdom of God, (CH 596) or The kingdom of God is justice and joy (CP 591)

Penitence
Jesus says, 'Repent for the kingdom of heaven is close at hand'. So
let us turn away from sin and turn to Christ, confessing that we
have failed to recognize and honour the kingship of Christ in the
way we have led our lives, and seek forgiveness.

Righteous God,
you have crowned Jesus Christ as Lord of all.
We confess that we have not bowed before him,
and are slow to acknowledge his rule.
We give allegiance to the powers of this world,
and fail to be governed by justice and love.
In your mercy, forgive us.
Raise us to acclaim him as ruler of all,
that we may be loyal ambassadors,
obeying the commands of our Lord Jesus Christ. Amen

A priest says

Almighty God have mercy on you,
forgive you all your sins,
grant you time for amendment of life,
and the grace and comfort of the Holy Spirit. **Amen.**

Acclamation
Stand

Let us give thanks to the Lord our God.
It is right to give our thanks and praise.

We praise you, great God,
for you are ruler of the universe,
and have sent your Son to be King of kings.
We rejoice that he has triumphed over all the powers of this
world,
and governs the nations in justice and righteousness.
We celebrate his victory
in his life, death, resurrection
and ascension to honour and might at your side.
By your Spirit, claim our complete loyalty,
establish Christ's rule in every land and in every heart.
Accept our homage
as we offer our lives in the service of Christ's kingdom.
He is Lord for ever and ever. Amen.

This song of praise is sung
Holy, holy, holy is the Lord,
holy is the Lord God almighty.
Holy, holy, holy is the Lord,
holy is the Lord God almighty:
who was, and is, and is to come;
holy, holy, holy is the Lord.

The Collect of the Sunday before Advent
Eternal Father,
whose Son Jesus Christ ascended to the throne of heaven
that he might rule over all things as Lord and King:
Keep the Church in the unity of the Spirit
and in the bond of peace,
and bring the whole created order to worship at his feet,
who is alive and reigns with you and the Holy Spirit,
one God, now and for ever.   **Amen.**

MINISTRY OF THE WORD

Readings

Psalm *based on Psalm 72 between readings, Jesus shall reign* (CH97; CP
490)

Scripture Song. *Tell out, my soul, the greatness of the Lord (CH 712; CP 362) or Jubilate ev'rybody (CH 701)*

Responsory
The Lord sits enthroned as king for ever.
The Lord shall give his people the blessing of peace.

The Lord shall give strength to all his people
The Lord shall give his people the blessing of peace.

Glory to the Father and to the Son and to the Holy Sprit
The Lord sits enthroned as king for ever.

The Sermon

RESPONDING

Affirmation of Faith
Let us affirm our faith in Jesus Christ the Son of God.
Though he was divine,
he did not cling to equality with God,
but made himself nothing.
Taking the form of a slave,
he was born in human likeness.
He humbled himself
and was obedient to death,
even the death of the cross.
Therefore God has raised him on high,
and given him the name above every name:
that at the name of Jesus
every knee should bow,
and every voice proclaim that Jesus Christ is Lord,
to the glory of God the Father. Amen.
based on Philippians 2: 6-11

Hymn   Rejoice, the Lord is King (CH 281; CP 563)

Prayers
Let us offer our prayers before God's throne of grace.

A brief silence

God our shepherd,
guide your church into ways of loving service,
that the blessing of your abundant life may come
to those who are hungry, sick, and in prison.

In your great mercy,
hear us, O God.

God of justice,
guide those who today bear the responsibility of government in
the nations
and make them responsive to your will,
that those who live in scarcity and distress may have their hope
renewed.

In your great mercy,
hear us, O God.

God of comfort,
uphold with the word of life all who are sick or in hospital
(especially...),
that they may give thanks to you.

In your great mercy,
hear us, O God.

God of grace,
bless this congregation, and our neighbours in other denominations,
that we may be communities of lively fellowship, service, and witness in this area.

In your great mercy,
hear us, O God.

God of resurrection,
bring us with all your saints to the promised day of judgment and
mercy,
before the throne of Christ our Saviour.

In your great mercy,
hear us, O God.

Rejoicing in the communion of all the saints, and as children of
the kingdom,
let us commend ourselves, one another, and our whole life to
Jesus Christ our Lord. **Amen**

A general collect
Lord,
in the vision of your heavenly kingdom
you reveal among us the promise of your glory:
may that glory be ours
as we claim our citizenship in the kingdom,
through Jesus Christ our Lord.

Gathering all our prayers and praises into one,
we pray as our Saviour Christ has taught us:
> **Our Father....**

Hymn   Lord, for the years (CH 81; CP 81)

GOING OUT AS GOD'S PEOPLE

Blessing
Christ our exalted King
pour on you his abundant gifts
make you faithful and strong to do his will
that you may reign with him in glory:
and the blessing of God almighty,
the Father, the Son and the Holy Spirit,
be upon you and remain with you always. **Amen.**

Let us go in the Name of Christ.
Thanks be to God.

20 FOR USE WHEN THERE IS A WORLD FOCUS

From suggestions issued by the Church of Ireland's Bishops Appeal Committee for focusing on the needs of the two-thirds world. At this service the collection will normally be for Christian Aid, TEAR Fund or for the Bishops' Appeal, the proceeds from which are channeled through such organizations. Illustrative material may be available to help make the Word more relevant to the twenty-first century.

GATHERING

Grace, mercy and peace
from God our Father and the Lord Jesus Christ
be with you all
and also with you.

Come, then, and see what the Lord has done,
what destruction he has wrought upon the earth..
**God makes wars to cease in all the world,
shatters the bow and snaps the spear.**   *Psalm 48:8,9*

Blessed are those who hunger and thirst to see right prevail:
for they shall be satisfied.   *Matthew 5:6 (REB)*

Hymn   All people that on earth do dwell   (CH 683; CP 369)

Penitence

What does the Lord require of you but to do justice
and to love mercy and to walk humbly with your God. *Micah 6:8*

Let us confess our failure to be channels of God's love, peace and
justice in a troubled and unequal world.

**Our God and Father,
we confess with shame that we have come short of your glory,
we have not done what we ought to have done.
We have remained deaf to the cries of our brothers and sisters
who hurt.
We have remained silent in the face of evil.
We have not spoken up for those innocently condemned.
We have failed to call for liberation of those who are oppressed.
We repent.
In your mercy forgive us.
Make us strong in the Holy Spirit to live for you
and serve all your people, in Jesus Christ our Lord. Amen**

One of the regular forms of Absolution is said if a priest is present.

Acclamation

God loves righteousness and justice:
the earth is full of the loving-kindness of the Lord.   *Psalm 33:5*

The Lord executes righteousness and judgment
on all who are oppressed. Alleluia.   *Psalm 103: 6*

Let everything that has breath:
praise the Lord. Alleluia.   *Psalm 150: 6*

Song of praise
Hail to the Lord's anointed (CH 125; CP 87) or Tell out my soul (CH 712; CP 362) or the Canticle, Magnificat

The Collect
The Collect of the day is said if suitable, or
God, the healer,
whose mercy is like a refiner's fire:
Touch us with judgment,
and confront us with your tenderness;
that being comforted by you
we may reach out to a troubled world;
through Jesus Christ our Lord. **Amen.**   *(Janet Morley)*

MINISTRY OF THE WORD

Readings
Those of the day if suitable or any two from:
Isaiah 58:5-10; Isaiah 65:17 - 66:2 ; Luke 4:16-30 or Matthew 25:31-45;
Philippians 2:1-11 or James 2:1-13

Psalm 82 or 146 or Hymn, The Lord will come and will not be slow (CH 140: CP 37)

The Sermon

RESPONDING

Affirmation of Faith
Let us declare our faith in God.

**We believe in God the Father,
from whom every family
in heaven and on earth is named.**

**We believe in God the Son,
who lives in our hearts through faith,
and fills us with his love.**

**We believe in God the Holy Spirit,
who strengthens us
with power from on high.**

**We believe in one God;
Father, Son and Holy Spirit. Amen.**   *(based on Ephesians 3)*

Hymn   When I needed a neighbour (CH 499)

Prayers

For the Church
God, whose holy name defies our definition,
but whose will is known in freeing the oppressed:
Make us to be one with all who cry for justice
that all who speak your praise may struggle for your truth;
through Jesus Christ. **Amen.**   *(Janet Morley)*

O God, you challenge the powers that rule the world,
through the needy, the compassionate and those who are filled
with longing.
Make us hunger and thirst to see right prevail,
and single minded in seeking peace;
that we may see your face and be satisfied in you,
through Jesus Christ. **Amen.**

For the nations and their leaders
Lord of the nations and friend of the poor,
strengthen in the leaders of today's world
   a belief in human dignity and basic human rights,
   a belief in the values of justice, freedom and peace,
   in love and generosity,
   in reason rather than force.
So may the nations grow in mutual respect and understanding,
and recognize that the problem of world poverty

is the concern and responsibility of all.
Grant this for Jesus Christ's sake. **Amen.**

Give us, Father, a vision of your world as love would make it;
a world where benefits are shared,
so that everyone can enjoy them;
a world where different people and cultures live
with tolerance and mutual respect;
a world where peace is built with justice
and justice is fired by love;
and give us the courage and the strength to build it;
through Jesus Christ our Lord. **Amen.** *(Women of Guatemala)*

Concluding prayer
God of righteousness,
lead us, we pray, in the ways of justice and of peace;
inspire us to break down all tyranny and oppression.
To gain for every person their due reward and from every person
their due service,
that each may live for all and all may care for each.
In us, through us, and if need be, despite us,
may God's will be done. Amen *(William Temple)*

Gathering up all our petitions and our intentions to serve the
needs of the world,
we pray as our Saviour Christ has taught us, saying,
Our Father .....

Hymn Brother, sister, let me serve you (CH 517; CP 393) or Make me a channel of your peace (CH 503; CP 519)

GOING OUT AS GOD'S PEOPLE

Lord Jesus Christ, you emptied yourself, taking the form of a servant.
Through your love, make us servants of one another.

Lord Jesus Christ, for our sake you became poor.
May our lives and gifts enrich the life of your world.

O God, open our minds that we may see
what you wish us to do;
and then give us the will, the courage,
the intelligence and the love to do it;
in Jesus' Name. Amen.

Blessing

May God the Creator who shakes the earth,
God the Redeemer, whom death could not contain,
God the Strength giver, who disturbs and heals,
the Holy Trinity of love,
bless you and give you power to go forth, proclaim the gospel
and fill the world with justice. **Amen**

Dismissal

Go, and God go with you.
In the name of Jesus. Amen.

21 FOR PEACE AND RECONCILIATION

In the long years of the 'Troubles' in N. Ireland one atrocity brought universal condemnation and pain. It happened in the Heights Bar in the village of Loughinisland which was within one of my parishes. On 18 June 1994 'loyalist' gunmen entered the bar and shot six men including an 87 year old man. They had been watching on television Ireland play Italy in the World Cup. A few weeks later I was invited to broadcast the morning service on BBC Radio Ulster from one of my churches. I decided that the Church of Ireland parish of Loughinisland was an appropriate venue and approached the Roman Catholic parish priest who accepted my invitation to make it a service for both congregations. The choirs of the two congregations practised together the music for the service, readings and prayers being shared. Canon Magee and I gave a joint blessing at the end of the service. The press were intrigued and one American asked how we could possibly worship together. I answered because we are Christians and neighbours. Three weeks after this broadcast service the IRA announced its 'cessation', and the beginning of the end was in sight. I include this not necessarily for use by others but to show how Service of the Word met an ecumenical and pastoral need at a crucial time.

GATHERING

Greeting
Grace to you and peace, from God our Father and the Lord Jesus Christ.
Thanks be to God.

Hymn   Praise to the Lord, the Almighty (CH 365; CP 558)

Acclamation
Stand
Bless the Lord, O my soul,
and all that is within me, praise his holy Name.

Bless the Lord, O my soul,
and forget not all his benefits.

Who forgives all your sin,
and heals all your infirmities.

The Lord is full of compassion and mercy,
slow to anger and of great goodness.

As far as the east is from the west:
so far has he set our sins from us.

Glory to the Father and to the Son, and to the Holy Spirit;
As it was in the beginning, is now, and shall be for ever. Amen.

The Collect of Trinity 12

Almighty and everlasting God,
you are always more ready to hear than we to pray
and to give more than either we desire, or deserve:
Pour down upon us the abundance of your mercy,
forgiving us those things of which our conscience is afraid,
and giving us those good things
which we are not worthy to ask save through the merits and
mediation of Jesus Christ your Son our Lord. **Amen.**

MINISTRY OF THE WORD

Psalm 23 *in a setting from the Roman Catholic repertoire*

First Reading   *2 Chronicles 7: 12-22*

Scripture Song   *Tell out my soul (CH 712; CP 362)*

Second Reading   *1 John 4: 7-12*

Hymn   *Be still for the presence of the Lord (CH 325; CP 383)*

Gospel Reading   *John 15: 9-12*

The Sermon *based on 2 Chronicles 7: 14 If my people who are called by my name humble themselves, pray, seek my face and turn from their wicked ways, then I will hear from heaven, and will forgive their sin and heal their land.*

RESPONDING

Stand
Affirmation of Faith

We affirm our common baptismal faith.

Do you believe and trust in God the Father?
> **I believe in God, the Father almighty,**
> **creator of heaven and earth.**

Do you believe and trust in his Son Jesus Christ?
> **I believe in Jesus Christ, God's only Son, our Lord,**
> **who was conceived by the Holy Spirit,**
> **born of the Virgin Mary,**
> **suffered under Pontius Pilate,**
> **was crucified, died, and was buried;**
> **he descended to the dead.**

On the third day he rose again;
he ascended into heaven,
he is seated at the right hand of the Father,
and he will come to judge the living and the dead.

Do you believe and trust in the Holy Spirit?
I believe in the Holy Spirit,
the holy catholic Church,
the communion of saints,
the forgiveness of sins,
the resurrection of the body,
and the life everlasting. Amen.

Prayers

Penitence

Scripture says:
If we say we have no sin we deceive ourselves, and the truth is
not in us. If we confess our sins, God who is faithful and just will
forgive us our sins and cleanse us from all unrighteousness.
1 John 1.8,9

Father in heaven,
we confess that we have sinned in thought, word and deed,
we have sinned against you and against our neighbours.
Father, forgive.

The words of our worship have been barren
for we have not sought to be reconciled with neighbours
from who we are estranged.
Father, forgive.

We have not acknowledged that we are all your children
and, if your children, then brothers and sisters in Christ.
Father, forgive.

We have not reached in love to the uncertain,
the lonely, the fearful and the angry.
Father, forgive.

We have held on to the certainties of centuries of division
and have not heeded your call to change.
Father, forgive.

Even when the words we have spoken have had the correct sounds,
inside in our hearts we have not loved our neighbours fully.
Father, forgive.

We have not made use of opportunities you have given us.
We have failed to be strong and courageous.
> **Father, forgive.**

Father in heaven,
in these and so many other ways we have fallen short of what
you expect:
as we turn to you
accept our penitence,
forgive us our sins,
turn and heal us we pray.
We ask this for the sake of your Son Jesus Christ our Lord. **Amen.**

Hymn   The peace prayer: Lord, make me a means of your peace. (John Foley)

Intercession

Almighty God,
you have promised that you will come near to us when we come
near to you:

We bow before you
and bring before you the needs of our world, saying
> Lord, in your mercy:
> **hear our prayer.**

We pray for one another as we meet the trials and testing of our faith.
In our pain, give us perseverance;
in our ignorance, wisdom
and amidst our doubts, faith.
> Lord, in your mercy:
> **hear our prayer.**

We pray for our families, neighbours and friends.
In our life together, give us love and humility.
Make us quick to listen and slow to anger.
Make us doers as well as hearers of your word,
and make us peacemakers, full of peace and integrity.
> Lord, in your mercy:
> **hear our prayer.**

We pray for those in need, inside and outside the Church.
for those who care for orphans and widows,
for all victims of violence, in this land and elsewhere,
remembering especially those who lost their lives in our parish.

We pray for justice in our society,
and for the capacity to love those whom we think are different
from us.

> Lord, in your mercy:
> **hear our prayer.**

We pray for those who govern and for the leaders of the nations...
for elected representatives of the people and all who influence the
thoughts and actions of others.
Set a guard over their words
and take away all violence and all that causes violence.

> Lord, in your mercy:
> **hear our prayer.**

We pray in faith for those who are sick and in trouble,
for all who live in fear.
for time to pray,
for people to pray with,
for prayer to be answered.

> Lord, in your mercy:
> **hear our prayer.**

Bring us together with the poor and all your saints
to inherit the kingdom you promise to those who love you.

> **Lord of the Church,**
> **hear our prayer,**
> **and make us one in heart and mind**
> **to serve you with joy for ever. Amen.**

A general collect

Almighty God,
from whom all thoughts of truth and peace proceed:
Kindle, we pray, in every heart the true love of peace;
and guide with your pure and peaceable wisdom
those who govern the nations of the earth;
that in tranquillity your kingdom may go forward,
till the earth is filled with the knowledge of your love;
through Jesus Christ our Lord. **Amen.**

Gathering all our prayers and praises into one we pray as our
Saviour Christ has taught us

> **Our Father....**

Hymn   *Be thou my vision, O Lord of my heart (CH 643; CP386)*

GOING OUT AS GOD'S PEOPLE

Responsory

Come, Lord Jesus, with healing hands, to bind us together in unity.
Take from us our words, which sound full of peace
But are only subtle weapons to separate us from one another.

Come, Lord Jesus, with healing hands, to bind us together in unity.

Take from us our fear that keeps us bound
Unable to reach out and comfort one another.

Come, Lord Jesus, with healing hands, to bind us together in unity.
(Diane Davis Andrew)

Blessing

May God the Father,
who made from one every nation on the earth, bless you.
Amen.

May God the Son,
who bought us for God from every tribe and language and
people and nation,
bless you. **Amen.**

May God the Holy Spirit, who brings us together in unity,
bless you. **Amen.**

Almighty God, bless you,
the Father, the Son and the Holy Spirit. **Amen.**

22 CELEBRATION OF A NEW MINISTRY
COMMISSIONING OF CHURCH WORKERS

This order was developed in a large parish for use in helping people entering new ministries to commit their ministry to the grace of God and to give a liturgical introduction to their ministry. It is informal in nature.

It is intended that the ministry being entered should be expressed in the context of the service, e.g. where a ministry of the word is involved, those being commissioned should read the word. Unlike most of the other forms in this book it has to be re-worked locally to suit the occasion.

Selected Bible Readings are given to reflect the diverse gifts and ministries which may be introduced. The readings of the Sunday may be preferred or other readings may be used. Hymns and scripture songs are included where appropriate.

GATHERING

Greeting

Grace to you and peace from God our Father and the Lord Jesus Christ
and also with you

Acclamation

To you, O Lord, I offer my prayer;
in you, my God, I trust.

Teach me your ways, O Lord;
make them known to me.

Teach me to live according to your truth,
for you are my God, who saves me. I always trust in you.

Remember, O Lord, your kindness and constant love
Forgive the sins and errors of my youth.

In your constant love and goodness, remember me, Lord!
Because you, Lord, are righteous and good.

From Psalm 25

The Collect

Lord Almighty, giver of all good things,
by your Spirit you have blessed your church with many gifts
to help us grow in grace and love:
Kindle in our hearts a ready desire to serve your purposes

and equip us with all necessary skills to fulfil your calling,
that we may bring glory to your Son
and build up your church;
through Jesus Christ our Lord. **Amen**

MINISTRY OF THE WORD

Readings   *One or two from the Old and New Testaments.*

A Psalm

Gospel Reading

A Scripture Song

The Sermon

Suggested bible readings for the following ministry areas are given at the end of the order.
The form used to present the readings and psalms (drama, music, spoken word etc.) is flexible. The Gospel should be read.

RESPONDING

Some of the following phrases are to be used and amended as appropriate to the particular ministry being celebrated. In each case a description of the main tasks anticipated, the connection with the ministry of all the baptized people of God and the support of the congregation should be expressed.

The Appointing and Commissioning

You have been duly appointed by the parish to serve as ...
Your brothers and sisters in Christ have come to support you as
you begin your new ministry here.

Your service is among people, especially ...,
so we encourage you to see them with his eyes of love

Your ministry is to the Church, especially in this place,
so we summon you to seek the well being of Christ's body in
whose name you work.

Your bondage is to Christ, who promises you his perfect freedom,
so we call you to give yourself wholeheartedly to the task he
gives you.

The ministry God calls you to fulfil is part of the ministry of all
baptized people.

So we invite you to seek the support and prayers of those who share with you the ministry of God.

We commit you to God's care.

A time of silent prayer

Relying on the mercies of God, and following in his ways
will you do your best to fulfil the calling you accept today?
With the help of God, I will.

Seeking to preserve the unity of the church, and the honour of Christ's name
will you submit yourself to those placed over you in this work?
With the help of God, I will.

Knowing the power of the Holy Spirit in your life,
will you work in his strength and witness to Christ's love in the way you serve?
With the help of God, I will.

Almighty God,
bless, preserve and keep you,
pour out upon you the riches of his grace
and settle you in the faith
for the glory of his Son Jesus Christ our Lord. **Amen**

Affirmation of faith

Do you believe and trust in God the Father,
creator of heaven and earth?
I believe and trust in him.

Do you believe and trust in God's Son Jesus Christ,
who redeemed mankind?
I believe and trust in him.

Do you believe and trust in the Holy Spirit
who gives life to the people of God?
I believe and trust in him.

This is the faith of the Church.
This is our faith.
We believe and trust in one God
Father, Son, and Holy Spirit.

Prayers

Let us pray

Lord, have mercy
Christ, have mercy
Lord, have mercy

Prayers may be led by members of the congregation, including representatives of those who will receive the ministry being commissioned and the leadership of the church. The content of the prayers should reflect the duties associated with the ministry(ies) being introduced.

The form of prayers may include the following responses.

Lord, in your mercy:
hear our prayer.
or
Lord, giver of grace,
mercifully hear our prayer.

The prayers conclude
And so, with all your people, we are bold to say:
Our Father.....

A hymn may be sung.

GOING OUT AS GOD'S PEOPLE

A concluding prayer

Renew us by your Holy Spirit,
unite us in the body of your Son,
and bring us will all your people
into the joy of your eternal kingdom;
through Jesus Christ our Lord,
with whom and in whom,
by the power of the Holy Spirit,
we worship you, Father almighty,
in songs of never ending praise:
Blessing and honour and glory and power
are yours for ever and ever. Amen.

Blessing

A suitable blessing brings the service to an end.

Suggested Readings

A teaching ministry (Sunday School Teachers, Lay Readers etc.)
Proverbs 2: 1-6; Psalm 25: 1-10; Romans 12: 4-8; Matthew 5: 1-16

A pastoral ministry (Parish Visitors, Child care, etc.)
Ezekiel 34: 11-16; Psalm 91: 9-16; James 1: 22-27; Luke 10: 25-37

A maintenance ministry (Church Sexton, Maintenance Team etc.)
Exodus 31: 1-11; Psalm 27; 1 Peter 4: 1-11; Matthew 6: 24-33

A managerial ministry (Select Vestry, Office Workers etc.)
Numbers 3: 5-9; Psalm 48; Romans 12: 4-8; Matthew 25: 14-29;

An evangelistic ministry (Mission Teams, Messengers etc.)
Joshua 1: 7-9: Psalm 40: 1-11; 1 Timothy 4: 6-16; Matthew 28: 16-20

A youth ministry (Youth Pastors and Workers etc.)
Ecclesiastes 11: 9-10; Psalm 119: 9-16; 1 John 5: 1-5; Mark 9: 33-37

SOURCES AND ACKNOWLEDGMENTS

This has been by far the most difficult part of this work to put together! For the orders of service in this book were compiled over a period of eight years, some by different people, none with thought of publication. In many the local leaflet will only have had the response printed. A good number of prayers were original but may have contained words half-remembered from a written source. The sub-committee of the Church of Ireland Liturgical Advisory Committee which produced the first sample orders certainly wrote from scratch in forms 1, 2 and 3 but included prayers from other sources. We sought and received permission to include them. One or two of the copyright holders no longer exist!

I note below the main sources. The publisher and I have sought to identify copyright material and are grateful for permission to use it. Should anyone recognize their material for which we have failed to seek permission we apologise and this will be rectified in any reprint.

Unless otherwise noted biblical quotations are from the *New Revised Standard Version* © 1998, 1995 the Division of Christian Education in the USA and are used with permission.

One quotation is from the *Revised Standard Version* © 1971 as above and one is from the *Revised English Bible* © 1989 Oxford and Cambridge University Presses.

Material from *The Book of Common Prayer of the Church of Ireland*, 2004 edition, (Columba Press 2004). © 2004 the Representative Church Body is used by permission.

Common Worship: Services and Prayers for the Church of England (Church House Publishing 2000) © 2000 The Archbishops' Council. Material used by permission. 4.21; 7.34; 8.45; 11.54; 15.85; 16.90; 18.102; 19.107

Common Worship: Psalter details as above. 2.14; 4.19; 12.58; 13.73

Patterns for Worship and New Patterns for Worship (Church House Publishing © 1989, 1995, 2001 Archbishop's Council. 1.12; 2.13; 3.16,18; 10.50; 11.63,64,65,66; 14.82; 15. 84,86,87; 18.100

Common Worship: Times and Seasons Report (Church House Publishing © 2003 Archbishops' Council). 11. throughout.

The Promise of his Glory. (Church House Publishing © 1991 Archbishops' Council)   6.26, 27*, 30, 31*, 32*, 35; 7.36, 37; 8.38, 40, 41, 42; 16.88, 90, 93; 18. 103, 104*. * indicates revised according to Times and Seasons Report 2004.

Episcopal Church of the USA. Book of Common Prayer 1979. Free permission to use acknowledged. 1.11; 2.15

Methodist Worship Book. © 1999 Trustees of Methodist Church. Used by permission 14.77, 78

English Language Liturgical Consultation. © 1978 and used with permission. Agreed texts of *Sursum Corda, Sanctus* and *Gloria patri*

Church Pastoral Aid-Society. Permission granted for original publication for material in *Church Family Worship* © 1988 Jubilate Hymns Ltd. 2.13; 3.17; 3: 18;5.25;13.76; 10.51,52; 15.83

Sundays and Seasons, annual volumes © 2001, 2002, 2003. Augsburg Fortress. Minneapolis USA. Used by permission. All rights reserved.
6.26; 8.38, 39; 9.44; 11.61; 12.67, 70; 13. 72, 73; 14.78, 82; 18: 100, 102. Mostly adapted to British Isles situations.

Edwin Le Grice. *Sing Together.* © 1992 the author. Canterbury Press. 1994. 12.69; 13.74; 14.79; 18.89

Society of Saint Francis. *Celebrating Common Prayer* © 1992. 4.19, 21, 22, 23

Services for Remembrance Sunday. © 1968 SPCK . 17. throughout

SINGLE QUOTATION:
Janet Morley, *All Desires Known* (SPCK 1992) 19.106
James Quinn, SJ   Source unknown   16.92
Diane Davis Andrew, *Cry Hosanna!* © 1975 Celebration Services (International) Ltd
E. Milner-White, *After the Third Collect* © 1959 Mowbray 7.35c
ICEL   *Opening Prayers.* Canterbury Press 1999. 6.31

Michael Baughen and Jubilate Hymns (permission for use given to me personally in 1993.) 4.20